Melanie Klein and Marcelle Spira: Their Correspondence and Context

Melanie Klein and Marcelle Spira: Their Correspondence and Context includes 45 letters Melanie Klein wrote to the Swiss psychoanalyst Marcelle Spira between 1955 and 1960, as well as six rough drafts from Spira. They were discovered in Spira's library after her death in 2006. As only a few of the letters that Klein wrote to her colleagues have been preserved, this moving, historically important correspondence enlightens the last five years of Klein's creative life.

The common theme of the letters is their discussion of the French translation of *The Psycho-Analysis of Children* by Boulanger in collaboration with Spira. The translation, first undertaken by Lacan, went through many ups and downs until it was published in 1959 by the Presses Universitaires de France. Klein also discusses her current work, in particular *Envy and Gratitude* (1957). She encourages her pioneering Swiss colleague Spira to be patient in the face of the resistance shown towards Kleinian thinking. Identifying herself to some extent with her younger follower, Klein reveals a very touching autobiographical account of the difficulties that she herself had encountered in her work and how she overcame them.

In *Melanie Klein and Marcelle Spira: Their Correspondence and Context*, Jean-Michel Quinodoz brings together these important letters. This rare collection of their correspondence is a valuable contribution to the history of psychoanalysis and will be essential reading for psychoanalysts, trainee psychoanalysts and lay readers with an interest in the work of Klein and Spira.

Jean-Michel Quinodoz is a psychoanalyst in private practice in Geneva. He is a member of the Swiss Psychoanalytical Society and a Distinguished Fellow of the British Psychoanalytical Society. He is author of *The Taming of Solitude* (Routledge, 1993), *Dreams That Turn Over a Page* (Routledge, 2002), *Reading Freud* (Routledge, 2005) and *Listening to Hanna Segal* (Routledge, 2007).

Melanie Klein and Marcelle Spira: Their Correspondence and Context

Jean-Michel Quinodoz

Routledge
Taylor & Francis Group

LONDON AND NEW YORK

First published in France 2013
by Presses Universitaires de France
6, Avenue Reille, 75014 Paris

First published 2015
by Routledge
27 Church Road, Hove, East Sussex BN3 2FA

and by Routledge
711 Third Avenue, New York, NY 10017

Routledge is an imprint of the Taylor & Francis Group, an informa business

© 2015 Jean-Michel Quinodoz

British Library Cataloguing in Publication Data
A catalogue record for this book is available from the British Library

Library of Congress Cataloging in Publication Data
Klein, Melanie.
[Melanie Klein. English]
Melanie Klein and Marcelle Spira : their correspondence and context / [edited by] Jean-Michel
Quinodoz.
pages cm
Includes bibliographical references and index.
ISBN 978-0-415-85582-2 (hbk)
1. Klein, Melanie--Correspondence. 2. Spira, Marcelle, 1910-2006. 3. Psychoanalysis. 4. Women
psychoanalysts. I. Quinodoz, Jean-Michel. II. Title.
BF109.K57A413 2014
150.19'5092--dc23
2014008556

ISBN: 978-0-415-85582-2 (hbk)
ISBN: 978-1-315-75663-9 (ebk)

Typeset in Times
by Saxon Graphics Ltd, Derby

To Danielle

Contents

Foreword

Ronald Britton

Though this book is presented with characteristic modesty by Jean-Michel Quinodoz, it is invaluable for those with an interest in the history of psychoanalysis and doubly so for those who have been informed and inspired by the work of Melanie Klein. We have to thank him not only for unearthing and publishing this cache of illuminating correspondence, but also for contextualizing it so very well. His introduction identifies who people are, how they are significant and what was taking place in the world of psychoanalysis at such an interesting and creative time.

This correspondence between Melanie Klein in the last decade of her life in London and Marcelle Spira, a young woman determinedly pioneering a Kleinian analytic approach in Switzerland, is moving, enlightening and historically important.

At the time of this correspondence Klein was well established in the British Psychoanalytical Society with a group of distinguished followers and adherents throughout the world. She had however many opponents both at home and abroad. Though her analytic experience and education had been in Budapest, it was in Berlin in the 1920s that her groundbreaking development of child analysis began. It not only started a new chapter in the understanding of child development, it also changed the analysis of adults and enlarged the patient group with whom it was possible to work to include borderline and psychotic patients. When Marcelle Spira trained in Argentina, there was a group there who espoused Klein's work, which included Spira's analyst Marie Langer, Enrique and Arminda Pichon-Rivière, Willy and Madeleine Baranger and Heinrich Racker. Spira was taken aback when she returned to her home country, to find that Klein's influence had not reached Switzerland.

Marcelle Spira was in her forties, much the same age as Klein was when she produced her highly original, controversial work in the 1920s, first in Berlin and then London. This, I feel, facilitated Melanie Klein's identification with this young woman who, alone and in the face of analytic opposition, was trying to introduce into Switzerland the Kleinian analysis she had learned in Argentina. Melanie Klein very much encouraged and supported her: providing her with personal clinical supervision and commentary on her psychoanalytic papers; and producing reinforcements in the persons of her two stalwarts, Hanna Segal and Betty Joseph, plus other visitors to her analytic patch in Geneva, such as Herbert Rosenfeld, Esther Bick, Donald Meltzer, Isabel Menzies and Hans Thorner.

What this correspondence reveals is a growing friendship from letters that begin, "Chère Madame Spira" and end with "Kindest regards", to those later that begin, "Ma chère Marcelle" and end "With Love, yours, Melanie Klein". There are 45 letters from Klein to Spira written in English and alas only six draft letters from Spira to Klein, written in French, as Klein did not keep professional/personal correspondence. Jean-Michel Quinodoz tells us Betty Joseph's explanation for this was her policy of protecting privacy.

What are also vividly revealed are Klein's professional preoccupations in the last five years of her life: five years in which she wrote *Envy and Gratitude*, *Narrative of a Child Analysis* and such papers as "Our adult world and its roots in infancy". Her concern that her work should gain recognition internationally is evident. She could not manage to journey to South America and therefore wrote:

> [I am] all the more happy that Dr Segal is going to work in the Argentine. In addition to her qualities as an excellent teacher and representative of my work, she has a very good command of French, which will be helpful.
>
> (Kl 37, 19 September 1958)

It seems that Klein herself was at home reading Spira's French while writing to her in English. Possibly English was not her second but third language. Being read in France in French is a preoccupation for Klein throughout the correspondence and the final triumph of a complete French translation of *The Psycho-Analysis of Children* is a touching moment. She wrote in May 1959, the year before her death, "it is the fulfilment of a dream that I have had for the past 27 years" (Kl 41, 1 May 1959). Jean-Michel Quinodoz tells us of the vicissitudes of the translation: its inception by Lacan; its continuance by Rene Diatkine and its subsequent discontinuance; its resumption by Françoise Girard, which was again interrupted by her premature death; and its final completion by her widowed husband Jean Baptiste Boulanger. Boulanger was French Canadian who trained in Paris and then resettled in Canada where he played a major role in the creation of the Canadian Psychoanalytical Society. He first heard of Klein's work at Merleau-Ponty's lectures in Paris and was enthralled. Lacan asked them to translate the second half of Klein's book and Françoise began this in 1954. Klein's international connections and interests are evident throughout this correspondence.

Klein's optimism in the face of opposition and rejection she transmits to Marcelle in whom she sees a fellow spirit:

> It is very difficult to stand by oneself, and it needs a great deal of courage and strength, but I believe you have these two qualities and therefore …you will

Acknowledgements and permissions

I would like to express my gratitude to my psychoanalyst friends and to all those, individuals and organizations, who helped to make possible this publication of Melanie Klein's letters to Marcelle Spira. The project was first envisaged in 2006, when the Committee of the Raymond de Saussure Psychoanalysis Centre in Geneva, through their librarian, Benvenuto Solca, asked me to study those letters with the idea of having them published. The letters had been given to him, with the agreement of Marcelle Spira's family, by her close friend Pierre Betout. My thanks also to Nancy Keller, who transcribed Klein's letters written in English, and to Mary Burzminski for re-reading my translation of them into French. André Haynal gave me invaluable advice on editing them. As a result of the information that my Canadian colleagues Marcel Houdon, Allannah Furlong and Jacques Vigneault were able to give me, I was in a much better position to understand the issues that Françoise Girard and Jean Baptiste Boulanger had to deal with as regards the translation into French of *The Psycho-Analysis of Children*, one of the main themes of that exchange of letters. Shortly before they died, both Hanna Segal and Betty Joseph told me how delighted they had been to read Klein's letters, for that correspondence reminded each of them of their meetings with Spira when she invited them to Geneva in the early 1960s. I would like particularly to thank Ron Britton, a distinguished representative of Kleinian thinking in contemporary British psychoanalysis; in his Foreword, he has found exactly the right words for sharing with us his feelings as he read those letters, which throw light on a particularly creative era in the history of psychoanalysis.

I would like also to express my gratitude to Kate Hawes of Routledge, who took the decision to publish the English version of this book, as well as to David Alcorn, who translated into English the first three chapters and the drafts of Marcelle Spira's letters from their original French. My warmest thanks also to Monique Labrune of the Presses Universitaires de France, who agreed to publish the French edition of this book.

The project received a very welcome grant from the Research Advisory Board of the International Psychoanalytical Association.

The London Institute of Psychoanalysis has authorized me to quote extracts from the article that I wrote under the title "Melanie Klein's letters addressed to Marcelle Spira (1955–1960)", which was published in *The International Journal of Psychoanalysis* in 2009 [vol. 90, pp. 1393–1418].

Cologny (Geneva), 7 April 2013
Jean-Michel Quinodoz

Chapter 1

The unpublished letters of Melanie Klein

In Marcelle Spira's library

Only a few of the letters that Melanie Klein wrote to her colleagues have been preserved. According to Elizabeth Spillius, who at my request examined the Klein Archives in London, there are letters that she sent to various members of her family, but no trace of those that she wrote to her colleagues. Only nine letters addressed to her by other psychoanalysts have been preserved. That is why I felt that it could be of some interest to publish the 45 letters that Klein sent to Marcelle Spira, the Swiss psychoanalyst, even though they do not discuss any very major psychoanalytical topics.

These letters were discovered in Marcelle Spira's library after her death on 1 April 2006, when she was 96 years old. She had bequeathed the contents of her library to the Raymond de Saussure Psychoanalysis Centre in Geneva (Quinodoz 2009).

Klein wrote these letters—all of them in English—between 1955 and 1960. Most of them were dictated by Klein and typed out by her private secretary; some, however, were handwritten from start to finish. Marcelle Spira trained with Kleinian psychoanalysts in Argentina and settled in Geneva in 1955; she held on to those letters and took great care of them. I have never seen them mentioned elsewhere, and Spira's name is not to be found in any biography of Klein (Grosskurth 1986; Segal 1979). The original versions of the letters that Spira wrote to Klein no longer exist. However, six rough drafts written by Spira, some of which are difficult to read, are still extant and are included in her collection of Klein's letters.

Everyday concerns

All through their exchange of letters, Klein discusses several topics simultaneously, or successively. The common theme has to do with the French translation of *The Psycho-Analysis of Children* by Boulanger in collaboration with Spira. The translation of that book, which was first undertaken by Lacan before he abandoned his attempt in 1949, went through many ups and downs; Klein's letters contain a lot of new information about what was going on between 1955 and 1959, the year in which the book was published by the Presses Universitaires de France. In her letters, Klein writes also of what she was, at that time, working upon, in particular *Envy and Gratitude*, which was published in 1957. These letters have often to do with practical questions, such as how she was going about organizing her summer holidays, which she frequently spent in a hotel situated in the mountains in the French-speaking part of Switzerland. A very discreet person, Klein rarely spoke of her family or of how she herself was keeping. As regards what interested Spira, this can to some extent be surmised from the replies that Klein sent to her and from the six draft copies of the letters that Spira wrote. On several occasions, Klein—at some length—encourages her younger colleague (Spira was 45 years old in 1955) to be patient in the face of the resistance shown by some of her colleagues in the Swiss Psychoanalytical Society towards Kleinian thinking. That enabled Klein to go into some very moving autobiographical detail about the difficulties that she herself had encountered and about how she overcame them.

Why publish these letters?

As to their psychoanalytical content, Klein does little more than comment on some papers that Spira was writing and wanted Klein to have a look at. Since Klein was too busy with her own work, she suggested that Spira come to London, where they could discuss these topics orally rather than send letters to each other. As far as Klein's personal life is concerned, the letters do not give us much more information than we already possess; there is indeed a kind of reserve on her part as regards her friendship with Spira. With that in mind, I would still argue that these letters bear witness to the final five years of Klein's life and to a decisive period in Spira's life.

As these letters are being published, it may be of some interest to think again, with Spillius, about why Klein did not hold on to Spira's letters or to those sent to her by other psychoanalyst colleagues.

"She [Klein] must have been assiduous about chucking things out." (Spillius 2006)[1]

There is probably the beginning of an explanation in what Klein herself wrote: as early as the third letter that she sent to Spira, Klein said that she would not communicate to anyone else the content of Spira's letters to her, if Spira so wished:

> I am always pleased to receive letters from you and I know that you will not expect me to answer them promptly. (…) I shall be very pleased to hear your opinions which you can express quite firmly to me and which, if you so wish, will not be communicated to anybody else.
>
> (Kl 3, 6 January 1956)

---

1 Personal communication by e-mail, 28 August 2006.

It would seem, therefore, that the fact that Klein did not keep any of her colleagues' letters had to do with confidentiality. One of my own colleagues, Dr Rolf Schäppi from Geneva, has confirmed that impression. His mother[2] told him that, as a young woman in the early 1930s, she had worked as a private secretary for a certain Mrs Klein in London and that Mrs Klein had instructed her to throw away all the rough drafts of her letters and other written work once they had been typed out, and not to hold on to them. Dr Schäppi was surprised to learn that his mother's employer was none other than Melanie Klein! And it was only then that his mother realized that she had been working for a distinguished psychoanalyst!

In some parts of her letters, Klein could be very critical of her colleagues or of psychoanalytical societies, and in particular of the Swiss Society. Uncompromising with respect to her own work, she sometimes made disparaging comments on what those who did not share her views—and perhaps even opposed them—were doing. That attitude is often found in pioneers who, in their desire to pass on their discoveries, are very careful to maintain their originality; this was the case with Freud, for example. Feeling herself to be protected by the confidentiality of a private correspondence, Klein no doubt felt that she could share some intimate thoughts which, during the lifetime of the people concerned, might have seemed defamatory. Now that more than 50 years have passed, what can we say about that situation? If we were still to maintain that confidentiality, would we not be depriving ourselves of an admittedly biased but nonetheless invaluable account of that exchange of letters, which the library of the Raymond de Saussure Psychoanalysis Centre in Geneva has made available for public consultation? In my view, now that a considerable number of years have passed, Klein's letters are no longer strictly private documents; their historical value is at present a significant element. I think that publishing them now may cast a new light not only on the way that Klein dealt with the reactions—often publicly quite disrespectful—to her work, but also on a turbulent period in the history of the psychoanalytical movement during which conflicts were certainly not few and far between.

Two witnesses of those days: Hanna Segal and Betty Joseph

I asked Hanna Segal and Betty Joseph to tell me what they thought of Klein's letters to Spira, because they had both been invited to Geneva by Spira towards the end of the 1950s.

I met Hanna Segal in London on 30 May 2011, just a month before she died. She told me that, for her, those letters were of historical importance.

> But I think it is a marvellous piece of research, extremely interesting. (…) For me, the most touching one was the last one, because I was there nearly every

---

2   Anna Schäppi-Wysling. Personal communication from Dr. Rolf Schäppi in Geneva.

day visiting Klein in the hospital. She was talking about her work and making sure that *The Psycho-Analysis of Children* was well edited.

(Segal 2011, interview 03:59)

Klein, however, never said anything to her about her exchange of correspondence with Spira: "It was not secrecy, it was privacy." The same was true of Spira: "She [Spira] must have been quite reserved… She was very careful of her privacy. I think she was right, it is [also] not secrecy, it is privacy. And she didn't speak much…" (Segal 2011, interview 32:50).

Segal did not remember a great deal about her few meetings with Spira, except for the time that Spira invited her to stay with her in her house on the Isola del Giglio, in Italy. She did recall, however, the importance of the Lausanne Symposium, which took place in 1956.

Klein was pleased that I was sent to it because I was "not aggressive"! [Laugh] And it was my first sort of public performance (ibid. 07:50). (…) This meeting was most important because it was the first common action; we all agreed about the importance of baby and child observation and the importance of child analysis. And we all agreed it was honesty, it was not compromise.

(ibid. 18:20)

I met Betty Joseph in London on 24 September 2011. She told me that reading Klein's letters reminded her of the first time that she stayed in Geneva, having been invited there by Spira. "Geneva was one of the first places I went to to give seminars and lectures: therefore I was very anxious and I must have been quite young." (Joseph 2011, interview 05:31) Did she remember Marcelle Spira?

She was a pleasant, easy person. She didn't talk much, and I was very junior. My impression is that she was an enterprising and brave woman, but hardly a personality to me. She [Spira] was quite reserved and I was very inexperienced and clearly anxious as to whether I could do good enough work. So I hardly got to know her as a personality. (ibid. 27:00)

In Betty Joseph's opinion, Klein was quite reserved in her letters to Spira, she was somewhat down-to-earth and revealed less of herself as a private person than one might have expected. I asked her if the reserve that Klein showed towards Spira might have been linked to the somewhat deferential attitude that Spira seems to have adopted towards Klein, as evidenced in the draft copies of her letters. Spira was probably overawed by Klein's renown—and that might have meant that she could not have a more relaxed and intimate relationship with Klein, whom she admired so much.

I think that is so… And also I feel that it was very brave of Spira to undertake the task of trying to help people to understand about Klein's work. But Klein was not a person expected to be idealized. People were in awe of her, but she herself had a great simplicity.

(ibid. 37:00)

Betty Joseph also recalled how demanding Klein could be with her close colleagues. However, in her view, in these letters Klein appears to be less demanding, although she does keep putting pressure on Boulanger and Spira to go on with their translation of *The Psycho-Analysis of Children*.

She was demanding, but I think we felt that it was clear her work came first, nothing would interfere with that, but that if one had such quality, really genius, one was justified in being demanding and apparently self-centred. We could put up with being a bit "bullied", or having to alter our papers, or being phoned and reminded that we must go to such and such a scientific meeting. She was so outstanding and this was part of what made it possible for her to carry on her work.

(ibid. 25:38)

Betty Joseph spoke also about the very particular situation in which Spira found herself in Geneva, where she was the only "Kleinian" psychoanalyst. Furthermore, it was very much the case at that time that someone who had not been analysed by one of Klein's analysands or by Klein herself was not seen by the London Kleinians to be truly "Kleinian". "Spira must have felt that she was the only Kleinian in Geneva, and so to speak the representative of Klein there, even though she had not had an analysis with any London Kleinian analyst" (ibid. 37:00).

Chapter 2

Melanie Klein, Marcelle Spira, Raymond de Saussure and the Swiss Psychoanalytical Society

Klein's life at the time she was writing to Spira has been well documented by her biographers (Grosskurth 1986; Segal 1979). I shall simply mention here what was on Klein's mind during the years when she and Spira were writing letters to each other; readers who would like more details about her life in the period between 1955 and 1960 will find them in those biographies. In this chapter, I shall present some brief biographical elements concerning Marcelle Spira and Raymond de Saussure in the context of the Swiss Psychoanalytical Society as it was at that time.

Melanie Klein (1882–1960)

In 1955, Klein was 73 years old. She was just recovering after a lengthy convalescence following on from an ear infection that caused her to have dizzy spells. She had to cut back her activities and had just moved into her new flat at 20 Bracknell Gardens in London—most of the letters that she wrote to Spira carry this address. In 1955, she was well enough to attend the 19th International Psychoanalytical Association (IPA) Congress in Geneva; that was where she met Spira for the first time. The paper she read, with the title "A study on envy and gratitude", would be published in 1957 as part of her book *Envy and Gratitude*.

In 1956, during the celebrations in London to mark the centenary of Freud's birth, Klein met Raymond de Saussure; he invited her to participate in a Symposium in Lausanne on the psychoanalysis of children. Klein said to him that it would be better to invite Hanna Segal rather than Paula Heimann to attend the meeting. The conflict between Klein and Paula Heimann had come to a head in 1953, but it was only two years later that their break-up became public knowledge. Klein told Spira about it. In October 1956, Jean Baptiste Boulanger gave Klein the first chapters of his French translation of *The Psycho-Analysis of Children*. Klein had promised that she would read each chapter as soon as it had been translated and in the years that followed she often encouraged Boulanger to press ahead with the translation. She was worried also by the fact that two other books of hers, *Contributions to Psycho-Analysis* and *Developments in Psycho-Analysis*, were running into difficulty as far as their publication in France was concerned. In

November, Klein invited Spira to London and asked her to work with Boulanger in translating the footnotes and index of *The Psycho-Analysis of Children*.

In July 1957, Klein attended the 20th IPA Congress in Paris, where she read a paper, "On the development of mental functioning", and took part in a discussion on the direct observation of children. After the congress, Klein spent the month of August in Château-d'Oex (in Switzerland) and was invited by Spira to stay in Geneva for a weekend. That year saw the publication of *Envy and Gratitude* and Klein began writing *Narrative of a Child Analysis*.

In 1958, Lagache informed her that the Presses Universitaires de France would not publish any more of her work. Klein encouraged Spira to have her membership dissertation for the Swiss Society published in the *Revue Française de Psychanalyse* or, failing that, in the *International Journal of Psycho-Analysis*. She was too tired to travel to Latin America, where she had been invited by Willy Baranger. Segal went to Argentina, while William H Gillespie and Paula Heimann were invited to Brazil.

In May 1959, the French translation of *The Psycho-Analysis of Children* was published. Klein was preparing the paper that she would read in Manchester University at a meeting of anthropologists and sociologists, "Our adult world and its roots in infancy". She attended the 21st IPA Congress in Copenhagen, visited her sister-in-law in Gothenburg, and spent her summer holiday in Wengen (Switzerland).

In January 1960, Klein congratulated Spira on the work that she was doing in Geneva, and finished writing *Narrative of a Child Analysis*. In July of that year, in the last letter she wrote to Spira, she said that she was delighted that Spira had finished translating into French *Contributions to Psycho-Analysis*. She added that she was in good health but that she sometimes felt tired—"which is not surprising at my age", she wrote. She spent the month of August in a hotel in Villars-sur-Ollon, in Switzerland. In September, she had an operation for cancer of the colon; she died in London on 22 September 1960 after fracturing her hipbone.

Marcelle Spira (1910–2006)

Back to Switzerland after training in Argentina

Marcelle Spira, a Swiss psychoanalyst and training member of the Swiss Psychoanalytical Society, was born on 19 March 1910 in La Chaux-de-Fonds, Switzerland. She did her psychoanalytical training in Buenos Aires and settled in Geneva in 1955. She retired in 1981 and died on 1 April 2006 on the Isola del Giglio, in Italy, at 96 years of age.

Marcelle Spira spent her childhood in La Chaux-de-Fonds. Her father Nathan Spira was spiritual leader of the Jewish community, her mother Marguerite was born Ditesheim. Marcelle studied psychology and married Paul Schwob, with whom she had a son, Gilbert. Some years later, she and her husband divorced. At the outbreak of World War II, she and her husband emigrated to Argentina. In

Buenos Aires, she was in contact with the principal representatives of Kleinian psychoanalysis there, in particular Marie Langer, her psychoanalyst, Enrique and Arminda Pichon-Rivière, Willy and Madeleine Baranger and Heinrich Racker. The remarkable development of psychoanalysis in Argentina during that period meant that Spira's training in child and adult psychoanalysis was particularly thorough. Years later, she would still say how much she appreciated the quality of the psychoanalytical training that she had received in Argentina, compared to what she had found in Switzerland when she went back there.

In 1955, the Argentinian government decided that psychologists would no longer be authorized to practise psychoanalysis. Spira returned to Switzerland and, after spending a few months in Neuchâtel, settled in Geneva. It was Raymond de Saussure, who himself had returned from the United States in 1952, who invited her there. Thanks to his excellent American and international experience, de Saussure had many ideas for developing psychoanalysis in French-speaking Switzerland and in particular in Geneva. In 1955, the French-speaking training analysts were Raymond de Saussure and Michel Gressot in Geneva, and Germaine Guex in Lausanne. Among those who participated in psychoanalytical activity were Lydia Müller, Marguerite Séchehaye, Marthe Burger-Piaget, Germaine Mercier and Laurianne Gressot. It was with the idea of strengthening that group that de Saussure encouraged Spira to leave Neuchâtel and settle in Geneva. "I'll be your Ernest Jones!" de Saussure is said to have joked to Spira (Spira 1996, p. 10).

Klein's concepts not well received

In spite of de Saussure's support, the fact that Spira belonged to the Kleinian school of thought meant that she was kept at arm's length—not to say rejected—by some other psychoanalysts, and in particular by those who practised child analysis. Melanie Klein's innovative conceptions were somewhat disconcerting because they upset the traditional ways of thinking of a section of the psychoanalytical establishment in the French-speaking part of Switzerland, who were influenced by some French psychoanalysts very critical of Klein's ideas.

In an interview that she gave to me in 1996, Spira spoke of the shock that she had on arriving in Switzerland in 1955: "The transference was hardly ever analysed—and certainly not the negative transference—and analyses were short." (Spira 1996, p. 9) She was above all surprised to meet psychoanalysts whose technique consisted in keeping silent, sometimes for a considerable length of time: "They would simply wait until the patient made his own interpretation." (ibid. p. 8) One day, she said to me, she retorted to René Diatkine, the Paris psychoanalyst, who had said that he could remain silent during sessions for more than a year: "You'll never make me believe that! I know you only too well," she said with humour. "You can't keep silent for more than five minutes!" (ibid. p. 16)

Spira was surprised by the disparity between the practice of psychoanalysis as she knew it in Argentina and the way it was conducted in Switzerland—and the converse was true also.

They were suspicious of me: I was a Kleinian, so they were against me. […]
I was the woman who wanted to eat everybody up, who was trying to seduce
them... All the same, their mistrust was not so much directed against me as a
person, as against the ideas that I had, those of Melanie Klein. They were felt
to be unscientific.

(Spira 1996, p. 6)

Some criticisms of Kleinian ideas were particularly disconcerting. In scientific
meetings, without even referring to what Klein had actually written, completely
wrong things were put forward in a very authoritative way. For example, one
rumour had it that Klein never mentioned the father's role in a relationship, only
the mother-child one—and that in spite of everything that Klein had written. Other
concepts were simply ignored, such as the early Oedipus complex, the depressive
and paranoid-schizoid positions, as well as the idea of projective identification.
That attitude of rejection has left its mark on some of our colleagues to this day.

Spira's enthusiasm for disseminating Melanie Klein's discoveries no doubt
meant that at times she would take things to extremes and perhaps even be
irritating; this probably made it difficult at first to enter into a dialogue. She told
me that a year after she arrived, de Saussure and Gressot approached her and
asked her to be "more Freudian and less aggressive"—and, if possible, to avoid
talking so much about Melanie Klein. "It would be much easier if you were to talk
a little less about Mrs Klein and spoke in a different tone of voice" is how Spira
recalls their conversation; "We are not against Melanie Klein, and you could hide
something of all that". That made Spira angry, and she replied:

As you can imagine, that is completely out of the question. It's a matter of
scientific honesty. If I talk about Melanie Klein, it's because she was the one
who invented the depressive position, not me! And I sent them packing!

(Spira 1996, p. 4)

When, towards the end of the 1950s, Spira wanted to present her work in order to
qualify as a member of the Swiss Society, she met with resistance not only from
her colleagues in the French-speaking part of Switzerland but also from some in
the German-speaking part, in particular the president of the society, Philip Sarasin,
in Basel.

Stay patient and pass on the ideas

Little by little, thanks to her hard work and perseverance, the early anti-Kleinian
opposition that Spira had encountered began to diminish. After a few months,
Spira began to analyse patients, to supervise the psychoanalytical treatment of
children, adolescents and adults, and to conduct a seminar on Melanie Klein's
contribution to psychoanalysis. Those who attended that seminar were trainees
and members of the society; Raymond de Saussure and Michel Gressot also

participated, thereby manifesting their interest in what Klein had to say (Spira 1996). Spira also gave seminars on the psychoanalytical approach to the Rorschach test; two of her students at that time were Mireille Ellonen-Jéquier and Terttu Eskelinen de Folch. Those lectures and seminars were instrumental in making both Spira herself and the Kleinian approach known to a wider audience. In 1957, Spira became a member of the Swiss Psychoanalytical Society and two years later a training analyst, after presenting a paper on memory. "Of course," she said, "I was not welcomed with open arms, far from it, but I was accepted, thanks to the work I was doing." (Spira 1996, p. 10)

At the end of the 1950s, when Spira began to take into analysis people wishing to train in order to become psychoanalysts themselves, issues involving seminars and above all supervisions arose—because an analyst cannot train his or her own analysands. These analysands could, of course, participate in the existing seminars devoted to the classical Freudian approach, but for those who wanted to learn more about the Kleinian approach, Spira was the only analyst who had the relevant expertise in this; there was no other Kleinian psychoanalyst in the society. Initially, therefore, Spira's analysands were allowed to participate in the seminar conducted by their own analyst, while some other solution was being sought as regards supervision.

Kleinians from London in French-speaking Switzerland

It was no doubt the meeting between Spira and Klein in 1955 that triggered the fact that Kleinian psychoanalysts from London were invited to come to French-speaking Switzerland on a regular basis in order to give lectures and supervisions. Hanna Segal was the first to be invited to take part in a symposium on child analysis along with René A. Spitz and Serge Lebovici.

That meeting took place in Lausanne in July 1956, at the initiative of Raymond de Saussure. It was the subject of several letters that Klein and Spira wrote to each other. On that point, Spira recalled an amusing incident that occurred during Segal's visit:

> Hanna Segal had agreed [to go to Lausanne] and she had found a camping-site where she could stay. Klein had written to me, begging me to tell Segal to wear stockings and iron her dress! When Segal came afterwards to my house, she told me to tell Melanie Klein [not to worry], because it was her husband who had packed her suit, wrapping it in tissue paper!
>
> (Spira 1996, p. 7)

Shortly after this, several other Kleinian psychoanalysts came to Geneva, one weekend per month, to conduct seminars and supervisions. Non-psychoanalysts could attend their lectures, while the supervisions were restricted to members of the society and trainee analysts, with each presenter having one hour in which to discuss a clinical situation. Feeling very much on her own, Spira had asked if she also could participate, but, so as not to make her own analysands feel uncomfortable, she did not herself intervene (Ellonen-Jéquier 2008). Thus it was that, in addition to Klein herself, who spent a few days in Geneva in August 1957, several psychoanalysts accepted Spira's invitation on many occasions, including Betty Joseph, Esther Bick, Hanna Segal, Herbert Rosenfeld, Donald Meltzer, Isabel Menzies and Hans A. Thorner.

Those regular visits by Kleinian psychoanalysts from London corresponded to Spira's wish to make it possible for French-speaking Swiss analysts to come together and develop their scientific discussions. Until then, the only encounters between French-speaking Swiss psychoanalysts were those that took place during seminars conducted by de Saussure, Gressot or Spira, in their own homes. Spira took it upon herself to organize meetings in her home that were open to all her colleagues; these became known as "Spira's Friday evenings" (Quinodoz 2006).

Finding her own niche and attracting a following

According to Spira, other psychoanalysts who were in tune with Klein's ideas were also keen on coming to Geneva in order to strengthen Klein's impact there, because they did not consider Spira to be really "Kleinian". Spira told me that, before she left for Europe, Willy Baranger had warned her that the only analysts who were considered to be truly Kleinian were those who had spent some time on Melanie Klein's couch or on that of one or other of her closest followers. She went on:

> Later, I realized that they came in order to try to convince me to undertake an analysis over there in England. But I wanted to work, not to start out on another analysis… That all fell apart somewhat, anyway, and when Klein died in 1960, I let the whole thing drop.
>
> (Spira 1996, p. 7)

As the years went by, Marcelle Spira gradually found her place in the Swiss Psychoanalytical Society thanks to her hard work, her clinical acumen and her passion for psychoanalysis—which she succeeded magnificently in transmitting to others. In one of the few written accounts of how things were in the late 1950s, Marcel Roch, a psychoanalyst from Lausanne, describes the change of attitude towards Marcelle Spira that occurred among Swiss psychoanalysts:

> Marcelle Spira was welcomed with the interest that de Saussure and Gressot had in the theoretical aspects of Melanie Klein's ideas and in those of the Kleinian school. We were, it is true, keen to know more about them, but at the same time we were quite baffled by them, for both theoretical and no doubt didactic reasons. At that time, working as we were in the context of Freudian metapsychology, it was difficult for us to imagine a way of teaching trainees about Kleinian theory too—all the more so, in fact, because we were very resistant to the idea of adopting Kleinian vocabulary without some

preliminary attempt at harmonizing the various concepts. So it was in a kind of "quarantine" that Marcelle Spira, after her admission as a full member of the Swiss Psychoanalytical Society, began her teaching. However, just a few years later, her seminars were included in the official programme. Co-operation and dialectical communication proved to be both stimulating and productive; they enabled every single one of us to benefit from what was a real "pathway" to a method of theorizing that remained open yet constantly challenged with respect to its manner of conceptualization and use in clinical and technical contexts.

(Roch 1980, p. 24)

Nowadays, we can say that Marcelle Spira had a wide following. Not only her many analysands in Switzerland, in other European countries and elsewhere in the world, but also those trainees whom she supervised and who benefited from her talent and profound clinical intuition can be counted among her followers, such as Danielle Quinodoz. I personally had supervision with Spira over a period of several years; she helped me discover the high quality of Klein's contribution to psychoanalysis and that of Kleinian analysts. In working with her, I became imbued, through identification, with what Spira used to call the psychoanalyst's "mental freedom". In her view, psychoanalysts should be as open as possible not just to verbal language, but also to non-verbal communication made of feelings, sensations and physical manifestations, and this towards both their patients and themselves. As the years went by, Spira was better received within the Swiss Psychoanalytical Society—she was its secretary under Michel Gressot's presidency. She was also one of the founder members of the Raymond de Saussure Psychoanalytic Centre, which was inaugurated in Geneva in 1973.

In Italy, Marcelle Spira was very active as a supervisor in both individual and group settings. She was initially invited by Franco Fornari to conduct seminars at the Milan Institute of Psychoanalysis from 1966 until 1969. Later, she supervised psychoanalysts from Milan, Turin, Florence and Bologna, some of whom went on to do a further period of analysis with her in Geneva.

A lengthy but active retirement

In 1981, Spira stopped working as a practising psychoanalyst. She spent her time in Geneva, in California and in her house on the Isola del Giglio, with her partner with whom she lived for many years, Pierre Betout. When she stayed in Italy, she continued her work as a valued supervisor with several groups who had regular meetings with her—even until one month before she died (Gregorio Hautmann, personal communication). From about 2000 on, Spira spent most of her time on the Isola del Giglio, where she died on 1 April 2006, at 96 years of age.

Spira felt very comfortable with individual and small-group supervisions. She did not like speaking in public or writing—indeed, her inhibition as regards finishing any piece of written work earned her an interpretation from Klein (Kl 36,

18 August 1958). She did, however, begin by having her translations of some articles published—for example, Baer's 1950 paper on the Rorschach test, and Klein's 1930 work on symbolism. She went on to publish several of her own papers (Spira 1963, 1966, 1983, 1986) as well as three books. In the first of these, *Créativité et liberté psychique* (Spira 1985) [*Creativeness and Mental Freedom*], she asked the question: "How does an interpretation come into a psychoanalyst's mind?". She replied by saying that, in her view, it was not a matter of inspiration but of freedom. That freedom lies at the origin of all forms of creativeness; it was one of her focal points all through her career and left its mark on her personality as a psychoanalyst. In *Aux sources de l'interprétation* (1993) [*The Roots of Interpretation*], Marcelle Spira developed her thinking on matters that she had earlier evoked. She emphasized the corporeal dimension of the psychoanalytical experience and the sensorial sphere from which psychoanalysts, like artists, draw their inspiration. Her last book, in Italian, was published in 2005: *L'idealizzazione* [*Idealization*]. For Spira, idealization is an inflexible defensive system set up in order to combat any awareness of separation anxiety. According to her, knowledge cannot do without the sensorial dimension, emotions or affects because without them there can be no true creative impulse.

Raymond de Saussure (1894–1971)

In this exchange of letters, Raymond de Saussure is explicitly mentioned—Klein writes about meeting him in London in 1956 (Kl 8, 8 May 1956); also, he appears implicitly, via the support that he gave to Marcelle Spira and to the development of psychoanalysis in Switzerland (Quinodoz 2005).

Raymond de Saussure was the son of the linguist, Ferdinand de Saussure. He was born in Geneva in 1894. After his medical studies, he was very quickly drawn towards psychoanalysis; at 25 years of age, he became a member of the recently-founded Swiss Psychoanalytical Society. In 1921, he went to Vienna, where he had analysis with Freud, then settled in Geneva. In the 1920s, he had a further spell of analysis, this time with Franz Alexander, in Berlin. He contributed greatly to making Freud's ideas known in France, and in 1926 he was one of the founders of the Paris Psychoanalytical Society, of the *Revue Française de Psychanalyse* and of the Congress of French-Speaking Psychoanalysts. In 1937, he left Geneva for Paris, where he had an additional period of analysis, on this occasion with Rudolf Loewenstein. In 1939, at the outbreak of World War II, he had to go back to Switzerland. In the following year, he was sent to the United States under the aegis of the Swiss-American Fund for Scientific Exchanges, and he remained in New York until 1952. He became a training analyst with the New York Psychoanalytic Society and an Associate Professor at Columbia University (Quinodoz 2005).

When he returned to Geneva in 1952, de Saussure put all his experience and dynamism into promoting psychoanalysis both in Switzerland and internationally. He initiated seminars in collaboration with Germaine Guex in Lausanne and

Chapter 3

From Lacan to Boulanger

It took ten years to translate *The Psycho-Analysis of Children* into French

"I still believe that the main book to be translated into French would be *The Psycho-Analysis of Children*."

(Kl 6, 29 March 1956)

In her letters to Marcelle Spira, Klein shows how impatient she was to have the translation into French of *The Psycho-Analysis of Children* to be completed, not only because she considered that book to be (for French-speaking readers) the most important of all, but also because, since she had a good knowledge of French, she wanted to check the translation herself. She told Spira that ever since 1932 she had been dreaming of seeing the book published in French; that dream was to be fulfilled in 1959, after ten years of trials and tribulations.

The translation into French of *The Psycho-Analysis of Children* is one of the main themes of the exchange of correspondence between Klein and Spira, but those letters speak only about the final five years of that laborious task. I shall therefore summarize what happened during the first six years of that work. It all began in 1949, when Lacan suggested that he could translate it into French, and ended in 1959, when the translation, which had in the meantime been taken up by Jean Baptiste Boulanger, was finally published. The years between 1949 and 1952 have been well researched both by Grosskurth (1986) as regards Klein and the Boulangers; and by Roudinesco (1993) as regards Lacan. All the same, neither biographer says any more about what happened after 1952 and there is therefore no mention of the subsequent vicissitudes described in the Klein-Spira letters between 1955 and 1960, the year in which Melanie Klein died.

From Jacques Lacan to René Diatkine

With Lacan, it all began in August 1949. During the 16th IPA Congress in Zürich, Lacan met Melanie Klein and asked her to authorize him to translate into French *The Psycho-Analysis of Children*. "[S]he was delighted when Lacan approached her on this occasion and charmed her into agreeing to let him translate *The Psycho-Analysis of Children* into French." (Grosskurth 1986, p. 377) According to Roudinesco, they both had reasons for moving closer to each other:

As for Melanie Klein, she was not interested in what Lacan had to say: she found it difficult to understand, untranslatable, and of little use to her. She was very much aware, however, of the help Lacan could be to her in France, and she knew how much he was admired by the younger generation. [...] Lacan, for his part, was still determined to get her support in promoting the idea of the "progress of psychoanalysis".

(Roudinesco 1993 [1997, p. 196])

Almost at the same time, one of Lacan's young followers, Françoise Girard, asked Klein for permission to translate the book; Klein replied that someone else was already working on it, although she did not mention who that person was. She advised Girard to translate *Contributions to Psycho-Analysis* instead.[3] When Lacan returned to Paris, he began translating *The Psycho-Analysis of Children*, but soon put it aside and asked René Diatkine—who at that time was being analysed by Lacan—to continue the work. When Diatkine finished translating the first part of the book from the German edition, Lacan asked to see the translation. Diatkine gave it to him, but Lacan never returned it. Unfortunately it was the only copy of the French translation that then existed. Two years later, at the Amsterdam Congress in 1951, Diatkine told Klein about what had happened.

The Boulangers take over the work of translation

Some months later, in October 1951, Lacan asked Françoise Girard if she and her Canadian husband, Jean Baptiste Boulanger, would like to finish translating into French *The Psycho-Analysis of Children*. Without mentioning any names, he told her that the first part had already been translated. The Boulangers agreed and, in December of that year, asked Lacan to give them a copy of the first part of the translation so that they could compare it with their own work and standardize both the overall style and the terms used. Lacan never acknowledged the fact that he had lost the manuscript, as Boulanger was later to say, quoted by Grosskurth. "It never was officially *revealed* nor admitted by Lacan that he had lost the translation made from the German by Diatkine, who had no copy of his work." (Grosskurth 1986, p. 390)

The Boulangers began to feel some concern over the fact that the first part of the translation had gone missing, and they went to London on 27 January 1952 to tell Klein what they suspected had happened. They and Klein immediately got on well together. They asked her to allow them to continue their work of translating the book from the English version and discussed with her matters relating to the translation of some technical terms and concepts. Grosskurth quotes extracts from two letters that Klein sent to the Boulangers in which she gives them her

---

3   That book, translated by Marguerite Derrida, was published by Payot in 1968 with the title *Essais de psychanalyse*.

opinion—proof, if need be, of the fact that Klein had an excellent grasp of the French language. In a letter dated 19 September 1952,[4] Klein wrote that, for the word "inside"—which the Boulangers wanted to translate as "*ventre*" [belly]—she preferred "*intérieur*". In the other letter, also written in September 1952, Klein explained the connection between Freud's interpretation of dreams and symbolism in children's play as being the equivalent of free association. She also emphasized the difference between envy and jealousy, suggested that it would be better to translate "splitting" by the word "*clivage*" rather than "*scission*", and advised "*réparation*" in preference to "*restitution*". Klein explains also that she "explained the difference between Freud's 'phallic woman/mother' (who has a phantasied *external penis of her own*) and her 'woman/mother with a penis' (*whose phantasied paternal penis is inside her*)" (Grosskurth 1986, p. 391).

Grosskurth says no more about the vicissitudes of the Boulangers' translation of *The Psycho-Analysis of Children* after the end of 1952; she takes up the story again in 1959, the year in which the book was published by the Presses Universitaires de France. She makes no mention of anything that occurred between 1952 and 1954—in particular the death of Françoise Girard in 1954, at 34 years of age, and Boulanger's subsequent work on the translation. In her biography of Lacan, Roudinesco also says nothing about all this. From that point of view, Klein's letters to Spira contain hitherto unpublished details about the final years of Klein's life and about what was preoccupying her at that time. In 1959, when, thanks to Spira, Klein learned that *La psychanalyse des enfants* had just been published, she told Spira what a tremendous relief that was for her:

> I was glad to see that it gave you so much pleasure that *The Psycho-Analysis of Children* has now appeared in French. To me it is a very great satisfaction—after all, it is the fulfilment of a dream that I have had for the past 27 years.
>
> (Kl 41, 1 May 1959)

Jean Baptiste Boulanger (1923–2000)

Since Klein mentions Jean Baptiste Boulanger, the translator of *The Psycho-Analysis of Children*, in several of her letters and since the translation of that book is one of the main topics in them, let me say a few words about the part he played throughout that period.

Jean Baptiste Boulanger, who was of Canadian origin, was a very important person in the field of psychoanalysis in Canada, particularly in Quebec. He was born in Edmonton (Alberta) on 24 August 1923 and died in Montreal on 30 July 2000. He was brought up in a trilingual environment, and this had a profound influence on his approach to psychoanalysis from a multilingual perspective. He

4   The Melanie Klein Trust.

was born of French-speaking parents in the western region of Canada, in an environment in which English was the prevalent language, and he learned Ukrainian from his day-carer. When in later years he was asked about his everyday bilingual (French and English) practice of psychoanalysis, he answered that he had never noticed any difference in the way French and English were employed (Furlong and Bienvenu 1994, p. 61). If there were differences within the psychoanalytical movement, he said, these had above all to do with the different schools of thought, not with the languages as such. In other words, in his experience, there was no difference in the way in which psychoanalytical ideas were expressed as regards the use of language, particularly with respect to English and French.

After his medical studies, Boulanger settled in Paris on two occasions in order to become more conversant with neurology, psychiatry and psychoanalysis. During his first stay there, from 1950 to 1953, he met Françoise Girard, a French psychoanalyst who was born in 1920; they married in March 1951. Like him, she had trained with the Paris Psychoanalytical Society. They decided to start translating *The Psycho-Analysis of Children* in 1951. At that time, French psychoanalysis was in something of a crisis. In Paris, Boulanger chose Maurice Bouvet as his analyst and was accepted as a trainee by the Paris Psychoanalytical Society. He was supervised by Francis Pasche, Maurice Schlumberger and Sacha Nacht. In 1950-1951, he attended lectures by Daniel Lagache, Professor of Psychology at the Sorbonne and in the Institute of Psychology of the University of Paris, and these made a considerable impression on him. Boulanger was kept up to date with developments in Jacques Lacan's thinking by his wife Françoise Girard, who was one of the few people authorized to attend the clinical seminar conducted by Lacan between 1951 and 1953. Although he did find Lacan's ideas interesting, Boulanger would later say that he felt no particular affinity with them. He was elected an associate member of the Paris Psychoanalytical Society in 1953.

It was when he attended Merleau-Ponty's lectures in the Sorbonne in 1950-1951 that Boulanger first heard of Melanie Klein's contribution to child psychology. "At that time, Melanie Klein's name had never been mentioned by any member of the psychoanalytical establishment in France." (Furlong and Bienvenu 1994, p. 60) He was immediately enthralled by his discovery of Klein's work—later, he would refer to this as his "conversion" to Kleinian thinking—and he decided that he would try to make it better known in French-speaking psychoanalytical circles; throughout his career this was to remain one of his objectives. When Lacan asked Françoise Girard in 1951 if she and her husband would like to translate the second part of *The Psycho-Analysis of Children*, it is therefore not difficult to understand the enthusiasm with which the Boulangers accepted the challenge. They left Paris for Montreal in the autumn of 1953, and played a major role in the creation of the Canadian Psychoanalytical Society. The untimely death of Françoise Girard on 6 September 1954 unfortunately put an end to their translation of Klein's book; Boulanger himself took it up again a year later. He stayed again in Paris between 1955 and 1957.

While he was living in France, the quarrels that occurred within the Paris Psychoanalytical Society made a lasting impression on Boulanger. This was particularly the case with the departure of Lagache and Lacan in 1953, when they created the French Psychoanalytic Society. "They were all at odds with one another, as though about to divorce!" (Furlong and Bienvenu 1994, p. 61) That was why, as soon as he returned to Montreal, Boulanger did everything he could to prevent such a divisive situation from occurring in the Canadian society (Boulanger 2000).

After the French translation of *The Psycho-Analysis of Children* was published in 1959, no further mention is made of Boulanger in the exchange of letters between Klein and Spira. He pursued a highly productive psychoanalytical career until his death in Montreal on 30 July 2000, at 77 years of age.

Chapter 4

Many common threads can be followed in parallel

Since each of Klein's letters deals with several topics, I have grouped together the main themes in chronological order, following these common threads: (1) the meetings between Klein and Spira; (2) Spira as translator of some of Klein's written work; (3) Spira's own writings; (4) Klein's on-going work, in particular *Envy and Gratitude*; (5) the trials and tribulations of a Kleinian psychoanalyst in the Swiss Psychoanalytical Society; (6) family news (of which there is little); (7) Klein's failing health; and (8) a self-portrait of Melanie Klein in her final years.

Meetings between Klein and Spira

Melanie Klein's letters to Marcelle Spira mention only three meetings that they had. The first took place in Geneva in the summer of 1955, during the 19th IPA Congress, which was organized at the initiative of Raymond de Saussure (Quinodoz 2005). Their second meeting took place in London in November 1956, Klein having invited Spira. The third was in Geneva in August 1957; Spira had invited Klein to visit her there. There may well have been other meetings during Klein's holidays—she enjoyed holidaying in Switzerland—in particular while she was in Château-d'Oex (Ellonen-Jéquier 2008).

> In the very first letter she wrote to Spira, Klein invited her to London so that they could have enough time to discuss in depth the technical and theoretical questions that Spira had evoked when the two women had met in Geneva: "I am sorry there was no more opportunity for a really good talk with you, but there never is at any Congress. Perhaps you will come to London sometime […]."
>
> (Kl 1, 21 October 1955)

One year later, as mentioned in her letter dated 12 October 1956 (Kl 12), Klein was again expecting Spira to come to London. In that letter, she thanked Spira for agreeing to translate the footnotes to the French edition of *The Psycho-Analysis of Children*. The following three letters are devoted to the preparations for that visit, which was due to last from Saturday, 10 November until Wednesday, 14 November

1956. The programme was as follows: on the Saturday, after checking in at the Cumberland Hotel, Spira and Klein were to have their first talk together; on the Sunday, Klein invited Spira to lunch, Hanna Segal would have a discussion with her in the afternoon, and Klein and Betty Joseph would join them in the evening; on the Monday, Klein invited Spira to present a clinical case to a group of five or six colleagues; on the Tuesday, her last full day in London, Spira would attend Segal's post-graduate seminar, supervision sessions and a lecture on child psychotherapy at the Tavistock. In a postscript, Klein wrote that Betty Joseph would take her place on the Sunday, apologizing to Spira for having to go to Cambridge that day to see her grandson, whom she very much wanted to see again (Kl 12, 12 October 1956; Kl 13, 29 October 1956; Kl 14, 2 November 1956).

One month after Spira's stay in London, Klein wrote to her to say how much she had enjoyed their meeting.

> It is not politeness that I reply that we were all delighted to have you here and were sorry you could not stay longer, nor it is *façon de parler* if I say that I am most grateful for the work you are doing and now in particular that you are going to take care of the translation of the *Psycho-Analysis of Children*.
>
> (Kl 15, 7 December 1956)

At the beginning of 1957, Klein asked Spira to recommend a good second-class hotel in the French-speaking part of Switzerland, a quiet one with a garden and deckchairs (Kl 16, 4 February 1957). She did, all the same, want Spira to enlighten her as to certain details that Klein felt to be very important, in particular her wish that her room should be no higher than on the first floor; this may have something to do with her fear, mentioned by Grosskurth (1986), of finding herself stuck on an upper floor if ever a fire broke out.

> Another point which I hope will be alright is that the room is not too high up. Of course, if there is a lift this does not matter, but if there is not it would be difficult for me to go higher than the first floor: in fact, I like being on the first floor.
>
> (Kl 15, 7 December 1956)

Klein stayed in the Beau-Séjour Hotel in Chateau-d'Oex from 2 August to 22 August 1957. Since Klein was about to spend a few days in Switzerland, Spira invited her to spend some time with her in Geneva on her way back to London. Klein was delighted, and said that she would stay there from 26 to 29 August 1957 (Kl 21, 21 March 1957). During her holiday in the Hotel Beau-Séjour, Klein asked Spira to have ready the footnotes already translated into French so that they could discuss them together and compare them with those of the English-language edition (Kl 27, 17 August 1957). As soon as she was back in London, Klein wrote to Spira to thank her warmly for her hospitality.

My thanks to you for your lovely hospitality you gave me are very warmly experienced. I enjoyed these days in Geneva and in your beautiful house very much indeed and I am going over the details in my mind with great pleasure and with gratitude both for your loyalty towards my work and, what is more, your real understanding of it and also – what I feel your warm personal feeling towards me which I value and reciprocate.

(Kl 28, 30 August 1957)

A few days later, Klein thanked Spira once again, saying that she now had a much better opinion of Geneva. "I keep a very pleasant memory about my stay with you and Geneva has now very much gained in my estimation." (Kl 29, 6 September 1957)

In the summer of the following year, 1958, Klein spent a two-week holiday in England and wrote to Spira from the Sandridge Park Hotel, in Melksham, Wiltshire. She was very pleased to be able to rest a little, and she managed to read a paper that Spira had sent her on "Psychological time"; she spoke very highly of it, as we shall see.

In 1959, Klein wrote only one letter to Spira apparently, informing her that she intended to attend the IPA Congress in Copenhagen. She asked Spira if she too was going to be there, together perhaps with her psychoanalyst friends from Geneva. Klein would then fly to Gothenburg to visit her sister-in-law,[5] and continue on to Zürich; from there, she would travel to Wengen, to spend three weeks holiday in that, not very high altitude, resort located in the Oberland region near Berne in Switzerland.

In 1960—she died in September of that year—Klein wrote to Spira saying that once again she intended to spend a three- or four-week holiday in Switzerland. She asked Spira to find her a comfortable hotel in a nice part of the country (Kl 42, 16 January 1960). Spira took so long to reply that Klein finally wrote to her saying that Eric,[6] Klein's son, had made a reservation for her in a hotel in Villars-sur-Ollon from 30 July to 30 August, as well as for her grandson,[7] who would be staying with her for the first two days (Kl 43, 17 March 1960). She replied also to Spira's invitation to stay with her in Geneva:

There seems unfortunately no opportunity to see you on my way to Villars. Perhaps on my return on 30th August? […] I very much hope there will be another occasion to see you. I am tired but not unwell and it seems that Villars will be a good place for a good holiday.

(Kl 43, 17 March 1960)

5   Jolan Vago (1884-1978), the sister of Klein's husband Arthur (Michael Feldman, personal communication).
6   Erich Klein changed his name to Eric Clyne in 1937 (Grosskurth 1986).
7   Michael Clyne, Eric and Judy Clyne's son.

A few days later, Klein apologized to Spira for taking the initiative in reserving the hotel in Villars, but pointed out that she had been waiting for several weeks for Spira to answer her previous letter. She added that her family did not want her to travel alone, hence the fact that her grandson would be accompanying her. That would turn out to be Klein's penultimate letter to Spira.

Spira as translator of some of Klein's writings

Translation issues are one of the main themes of Klein's letters to Spira, starting with the very first one in October 1955 and going all the way through to the last letter she sent in July 1960. I shall not enter into too much detail, because the problems mentioned are many and complex. First, there was the matter of Klein's *Contributions to Psycho-Analysis* which Spira had begun to translate on her own initiative, before she had even met Klein. Thereafter, Klein asked Spira to translate into French the footnotes and indexes of *The Psycho-Analysis of Children*, since Jean Baptiste Boulanger was finding it difficult to translate that book without help.

The exchange of letters between Klein and Spira highlights two main aspects. There is, first of all, the fact that Klein was particularly keen on revising— herself—chapter by chapter the translation of her writings into French, working closely with her translators. The priority she gave to the French translation of *The Psycho-Analysis of Children* was due to the fact that she considered that book to be her most important work, more important, for example, than *New Directions in Psycho-Analysis* and *Contributions to Psycho-Analysis*. In addition, the letters that Klein wrote to Spira fill the gap left by her biographers between Boulanger's resumption of the translation in 1954, and 1959, the year when the book finally appeared in print.

It was during their very first meeting in Geneva in 1955 that Spira told Klein that she was translating *Contributions to Psycho-Analysis* into French. Klein was surprised to learn that Spira was already halfway through the book and told Spira that she would like to revise the translation herself; she suggested that Spira come to London to talk things over (Kl 2, 18 November 1955). Spira, however, declined that invitation because she did not at that point have enough free time. Klein emphasized how important it was for her to have her papers translated into French.

> It is difficult to explain how much I have at heart the translation into French of my books, and it may give you an idea when I say that since 1932 I have aimed at getting my books translated into French, which seems to me so important and I am very happy to think that these plans are now on the way to being realised.
>
> (Kl 3, 6 January 1956)

In her next letter, Klein wrote that she was satisfied with the translation of the chapters from the *Contributions* book that Spira had sent her (Kl 5, 16 March 1956). Writing of the translation of her work into other languages, Klein said that she was delighted that Willy Baranger had, in Uruguay, translated *Contributions* into Spanish and that Professor Servadio was thinking of translating some of her writings into Italian. The translation into French of *The Psycho-Analysis of Children* having come to a halt after the death in 1952 of Françoise Girard, Dr Jean Baptiste Boulanger's wife, some five years previously, Klein hoped that Boulanger would be able to complete the work; if not, she would have to find another translator (Kl 6, 29 March 1956).

Klein's handwritten letter to Spira dated 5 October 1956 (Kl 11) is a cry for help; she wanted Spira to assist Boulanger in finishing the translation of *The Psycho-Analysis of Children* by the end of 1956 at the latest. Boulanger was trying to find someone who could translate the footnotes to that book. Klein asked Spira because she appreciated the latter's interest in translation and, saying that she was sorry to have to ask her to do this additional work, suggested that for the time being Spira stop working on the translation of the *Contributions* book. In the next letter she wrote, on 12 October 1956 (Kl 12), Klein said that she was very grateful to Spira for having accepted. It is to be noticed that henceforth Klein begins her letters with "Dear Marcelle" instead of "Dear Madame Spira". She added that Boulanger was delighted at the idea of working with Spira and that he hoped that Daniel Lagache would publish the book in the summer of 1957. We learn later that Boulanger was unable to keep to his timetable, so that he did not send his translation of the final chapters by the end of 1956 as he had promised. Klein made no secret of her irritation and impatience; she even thought of asking Spira to take over the whole of the work that remained to be done.

> I have not heard from Boulanger and I think there cannot be a hope that this man is going to finish the translation. […] I think I shall have to tell him that I cannot wait any longer. […] I feel […] I shall write to him that I would wish you to finish the translation.
>
> (Kl 15, 7 December 1956)

Annexed to Klein's letter dated 4 February 1957 are her replies to the questions that Boulanger had asked her. In her view, it was extremely important to differentiate between the phases of child development by using different terms in French for very young infants as compared to older children: depending on the context, "*bébé*" (baby), "*jusqu'à deux ans*" (under-twos), "*jusqu'à trois ans*" (under-threes), "*petits enfants*" (little children) or "*enfants en bas âge*" (young infants) would be acceptable too, as long as they were not used too often. She agreed with the idea of "*figure composite des parents*" (combined parents), as well as that of "*sadique oral*" (oral-sadistic), but preferred "*morcellement*" to "*fragmentation*" as a translation of "splitting".

> The question of describing the oral stage is more complicated. I agree to the use of "le stade oral de succion" and "le stade oral de morsure" wherever I refer to the oral sucking and the oral biting stage, but wish the expression

"sadique oral" and "sadique-uréthral" to be used wherever I refer to these in the original.

(Kl 18, copy of 4 February 1957)

Over one month later, on 21 March 1957, Klein again asked Spira to help with translating the index of *The Psycho-Analysis of Children*, since Boulanger had not at that point managed to finish his translation of Chapter XI. In Klein's view, that would enable him to complete his translation of that chapter, so that she could then revise it—once again she emphasized how important it was for her to do any revisions herself to the French edition.

> I am coming with another S.O.S. [...] Now could you make this new sacrifice and translate the Index? [...] It is the one I decided to revise myself, [...] but since it is my fundamental book and, years ago, I promised the Boulangers I would revise it, I felt I must keep my promise. It is an enormous relief to have the translation finished, which in fact has taken longer than the actual writing of the book, but it is extremely difficult to translate and Boulanger has done it very well. I am quite sure that later on it will be immaterial to me that it took a year longer, because it is the quality of the translation which counts.

(Kl 21, 21 March 1957)

On 9 May 1957, Klein wrote to Spira that she was very concerned about the index, since it would not be enough simply to translate it from the English or German versions. She wondered whether it might not be better to get a professional person to do that—but at the same time she realized that the latter would not be familiar enough with her work, the main reason for her always asking someone sufficiently cognizant with her approach to handle such a task. In the end, in a letter that Klein wrote to Spira, we read that the latter had indeed finished the index and that Klein was happy to revise it (Kl 24, 16 May 1957). She also revised the end of Chapter XI, once Boulanger gave it to her. In a short note dated 20 July 1957 (Kl 26), Klein wrote that Boulanger had agreed to send the completed manuscript of *La psychanalyse des enfants* to the publisher by 10 August. She thanked Spira for her work on the footnotes and the index.[8]

In a letter dated 17 August 1956 (Kl 27), Klein wrote that she would like to take advantage of the fact that she would be visiting Geneva in order to compare the index of *La psychanalyse des enfants* with that of the original English version. Klein was not happy with the one in the latter edition; in order to forestall any fear that Spira might have that this additional phase might mean that publication would have to be postponed, Klein reassured her that that would not in fact be the case.

---

8   In his "translator's note", Boulanger (1959) thanks Marcelle Spira for her translation of the footnotes and for her help in preparing the index (see the footnote for Kl 39, 3 October 1958).

In the series of letters that followed, we can catch a glimpse of the difficulties that *La psychanalyse des enfants* thereafter encountered. It had been accepted, along with *Contributions to Psycho-Analysis* and *Developments in Psycho-Analysis*, for publication in France. The work to be done involved not only Boulanger and Spira, but also Baranger as translator and Lagache, with whom Klein was often in contact with a view to finding an appropriate publisher. Since it would be somewhat tiresome to go into all the details of these various negotiations and developments, I shall simply summarize them.

With the Presses Universitaires de France about to publish *La psychanalyse des enfants*, the question arose as to which publisher might agree to handling the other two books. Spira was already working on her translation of the *Contributions* book, while Baranger was translating *Developments* (Kl 30, 25 October 1957). Lagache informed Klein that the Presses Universitaires de France would also be prepared to publish the latter two books, but not before two or three years. Klein thereupon wrote to Spira: "I do not feel that at my age I should agree to the translations appearing in 2 or 3 years' time." (Kl 30, 25 October 1957)

She then authorized Spira to contact another publisher, Payot, in her name and, in a letter dated 10 January 1958, she gave the addresses of another two publishers in Paris, L'Arche and Desclée de Brouwer (Kl 32, 10 January 1958). She advised Spira to be cautious in her approach: "Although Lagache says that my name is known in France, my impression is that it is not particularly known to publishers. So you have to go carefully about such an approach so as not to get another refusal." (Kl 33, 31 January 1958)

In the meantime, Lagache's discussions with the Presses Universitaires de France continued to meet with a point-blank refusal as regards Klein's two other books. At the same time, Klein voiced her surprise at how long it was taking for *La psychanalyse des enfants* to appear in print. She was later to learn that the Presses Universitaires de France had never received the contract that Boulanger was supposed to sign with them—it had been lost in the post because Boulanger had omitted to tell the publisher of his change of address in Montreal! It was all cleared up in the end, however, and a new contract was signed. On 1 May 1959 (Kl 41), Klein could at last take pleasure in seeing *La psychanalyse des enfants* published in France.

There remained the question of the translations into French of the *Contributions* and *Developments* books. In her penultimate letter to Spira, dated 25 March 1960 (Kl 44), Klein wrote of her delight that Baranger had almost finished translating *Developments*, and in the last letter that she wrote to Spira, on 1 July 1960, Klein said that she was very pleased to learn that Spira had finished translating the *Contributions* book. Those two books, unfortunately, would not be published in French until several years after Klein's death: *Developments* in 1966 by the Presses Universitaires de France with the title *Développements de la psychanalyse*, translated by Baranger, while *Contributions* was published in French in 1968 by Payot with the title *Essais de psychanalyse*, translated by the psychoanalyst

Marguerite Derrida, the wife of the philosopher Jacques Derrida. I do not know why Spira's translation was turned down.

Klein comments on Spira's own writings

From the beginning of their exchange of letters, Marcelle Spira put some questions about her own psychoanalytic work to Melanie Klein; from time to time, in fact, she sent Klein copies of her writings in order to seek her opinion. In several of her letters, Klein wrote that she was delighted to discover in Spira a colleague who was able to grasp her ideas with so much insight and depth of feeling. However, after a few written comments on issues that Spira brought up, Klein gave up the idea of written discussions because these proved to be too time-consuming. She therefore suggested that Spira come to visit her in London. Their few meetings together gave both of them the opportunity to enter into scientific discussions; Klein alluded to these from time to time in her letters, as we shall see.

In her second letter to Spira, dated 18 November 1955 (Kl 2), Klein said that she had just finished reading the paper on memory and the depressive position that Spira had read at the Geneva Congress some months before, with the title "Division of memory, depressive position, and their expression in the course of transference".[9] Klein found that paper very interesting and appreciated the originality of some of Spira's ideas.

> I was also gratified to find that you seemed to have very well understood my concepts. If there is anything I would suggest it is that it might be helpful if you describe the paranoid-schizoid position (to which you refer) in a similar way as you define the depressive position because some of the conclusions you draw as regards memory I would also consider from the angle of the splitting processes in the first few months of life. The importance of projective identification in the patient you describe seems to me very great and it might be worthwhile to connect your conclusions with this concept as well. On the whole I enjoyed your Paper very much and was pleased to meet a colleague who could look so deeply.
>
> (Kl 2, 18 November 1955)

Some six weeks later, 6 January 1956 (Kl 3), Klein wrote that the letter that Spira had just sent her was very interesting, particularly when Spira spoke of the necessary regression that we see in artists. On that point, Klein mentioned that Segal had written a paper with the title "A psychoanalytical approach to aesthetics" (Segal 1952), which apparently Spira had not read. In that letter too, Klein further developed what she had written in her previous letter about the importance of the paranoid-schizoid position.

---

9   This is the title given by Eissler (1956). A revised version was published later (Spira 1959).

To return to the point I made in my last letter – the importance of the para-noid-schizoid position which I have recently linked with excessive envy. It is in this position that the basis for insanity lies, and so much depends on how far it can be modified in the course of development or of analysis. In the book which I am now writing, the enlarged version of my Congress Paper, I made a particular point that excessive envy indicates particularly strong schizoid and paranoid trends.

(Kl 3, 6 January 1956)

In her following letter, dated 13 February 1956 (Kl 4), Klein wrote that she was very interested in the developments that Spira had talked about, but that she did not feel that she was ready to respond in any detailed manner. She promised Spira that she would send her a longer version of the paper she [Klein] had read at the 1955 Geneva Congress, the version that she had just read to the British Society.[10]

One year went by before Klein again wrote to Spira; they once more discussed the work that Spira was doing at that point. During that year, 1956, Spira had travelled to London in November; the discussions that she had had with Klein were not limited to matters of translation, but involved Spira's own work. In the letter she wrote to Spira on 22 February 1957 (Kl 19), Klein mentioned two articles that Spira had sent her. The first, which Klein could not remember particularly well, was a development of the paper that Spira had read at the 1955 Congress (Spira 1959). Klein did remember, however, advising Spira to send it to the *International Journal of Psycho-Analysis*. The second paper was, in fact, an older text, and Klein suggested that Spira revise it, taking her more recent ideas into account, whereupon Klein would tell her what she thought of it.[11]

Another year went by before Klein again wrote to Spira (Kl 33, 31 January 1958) about the latter's 1955 Congress paper. Klein felt that it would be better if Spira had it published in the *Revue Française de Psychanalyse*, but she was afraid that her own quarrels with Lagache might cause Spira some difficulty.

Should the *Revue Française de Psychanalyse* not accept the paper, then it should have to be published by the *International Journal of Psycho-Analysis*, but needs a really good translation. [...] Of course, the translation into English is not as useful to you in Switzerland as a French publication, in the official review, but, on the other hand, it would introduce you to the English and American public, so that I am not sure that it would be such a disadvantage.

(Kl 33, 31 January 1958)

---

10 "A study on envy and gratitude", in which Klein presents envy as being constitutionally linked to the death drive (Grosskurth 1986). It was on the basis of that paper that she would go on to write *Envy and Gratitude* (Klein 1957).

11 That paper was probably "Some aspects of the analysis of an epileptic boy", which Spira read to the Argentine Psychoanalytic Association in 1954 (Eissler 1954) and was later published in Italian (Spira 1966).

On 18 August 1958, Klein wrote to Spira from the Sandridge Park Hotel in Melksham, where she was holidaying. She had at last managed to read "Psychological time", the title that Spira had given to the most recent version of her 1955 Congress paper. Klein wrote that she had read the paper several times with a great deal of pleasure, and again tried to persuade Spira to have it published. In addition—an indication, perhaps, of a certain lack of patience on her part—Klein offered an interpretation concerning Spira's reluctance to see her work in print.

> Some of your ideas I remembered well from our conversation (when I stayed with you in Geneva) but I found them enriched and very well presented, illustrated as they are by good clinical instances. It is an excellent and interesting paper and gave me much pleasure. I wonder how and when you are going to publish it? You mention that you are going to enlarge it—is that what prevents you from publication? Or have you already taken steps to have it published? I should be glad to see this paper or your Geneva Congress paper published (of course translated) in the Int. Journal of Ps.A.—I remember we spoke about this but I don't know what you decided in the end. [...] You seem to be full of interesting and fruitful thoughts which should be experienced and published.
>
> (Kl 36, 18 August 1958)

In the end, some five weeks later, Klein wrote to Spira to say how pleased she was to learn that the *Revue Française de Psychanalyse* had accepted for publication her congress paper (Spira 1959). All the same, she added, it might take quite some time before it actually appeared in print... That letter, dated 26 September 1958 (Kl 38) was the last to include any reference to Spira's own work.

The period when Klein was writing *Envy and Gratitude*

In most of the letters that she wrote to Spira, Klein spoke of the books or articles on which she was working at the time; this was particularly true of *Envy and Gratitude* and *Narrative of a Child Analysis*. On several occasions she said how important her writing was for her, because putting her ideas down on paper helped her to face up to the criticisms that her detractors levelled at her. Through her letters to Spira, we can see how her work was progressing, we can guess at the happiness or disquiet she felt depending on the reception given to her papers and articles, and have some idea of the satisfaction she experienced whenever a reviewer praised her work in no uncertain terms. Klein had a good knowledge of French—it was in French that Spira wrote to her—and often said to Spira how important it was for her to see her work published in France.

It was in her fifth letter to Spira, dated 16 March 1956 (Kl 5), that Klein mentioned for the first time the importance that she attached to writing. She was, at that point, writing *Envy and Gratitude* and regretted that her other activities were paying the price: letter-writing, translation, etc. Two weeks later, Klein enclosed with her letter a copy of an unsigned review of *New Directions in Psycho-Analysis*, published in the *Times Literary Supplement*, 23 March 1956. Klein was particularly proud of this and explained why to Spira:

> I must explain that a review in this Journal is thought by literary people to come next in importance to the Bible, and the importance of such a review can be gathered by the fact that Dr. Jones explained to me, when I first came to England, that should I get a review in the Supplement, one should not mind unfavourable comment but measure it in inches.
>
> (Kl 6, 29 March 1956)

Two months later, Klein wrote that her work was progressing and that she felt much better.

> My book is advancing but until I have really got it to the publishers I shall not feel relieved from that burden. At the same time, I do not feel dissatisfied with this book, which could be vastly expanded if I put in more of my experiences but I feel for the purpose I wanted, it is probably better to leave it as it is.
>
> (Kl 7, 3 May 1956)

Some ten months went by before Klein again mentioned what she was then writing. On 4 February 1957, she told Spira that she was expecting the proofs of *Envy and Gratitude* to arrive at any moment; she would have them corrected by friends of hers in addition to doing her own correcting. She mentioned too that she had begun writing *Narrative of a Child Analysis* and that she had received the chapters of the French translation of *The Psycho-Analysis of Children* that Boulanger had sent to her. On the twenty-second of that month, Klein told Spira that *Envy and Gratitude* would be published within the following few weeks and that she had a new project for the 20th IPA Congress to be held in Paris later that year.

> I have announced a Congress paper with a splendid title "On the Development of Mental Functioning", and am quite afraid of what I am undertaking. After Easter I must stop everything in order to produce a paper which is worthy of the title *or at best not quite unworthy of it* [handwritten].
>
> (Kl 19, 22 February 1957)

The intense concentration that that paper demanded of her exhausted her, however, so that she had to put aside some other urgent tasks: "Before the Congress I shall get very tired because I am working extremely hard on my paper which I am finding difficult and I shall have to write and re-write it several times." (Kl 21, 21 March 1957)

During that same period, Klein wrote of her regret at not being able to devote more time to reading a paper that Spira had sent to her or to revising the chapters that Boulanger had brought to her in London: "I am deeply immersed in my Congress paper and the contribution I have promised to make to the discussion on the Direct Observation of the Child." (Kl 22, 5 April 1957)

On 21 June 1957, Klein wrote that she was delighted by the comments that Spira had made after reading *Envy and Gratitude*.

> You have given me great pleasure indeed by your letter, because it showed a deep understanding of something in my work and attitude which I think very few people would particularly connect with this book. I am also very glad to see that you use it already in your work [...].
>
> (Kl 25, 21 June 1957)

On 20 July 1957, Klein told Spira that she had at last finished writing her congress paper (Klein 1958). She felt exhausted and had no idea whether it was a good paper or not. All that remained was for her to write up some notes on child observation. When she returned to London after her holiday in Wengen (Switzerland), Klein sent Spira copies of the two reviews of *Envy and Gratitude*, one by Jean Howard in *The Spectator* (Howard 1957), and the other, unsigned, in *The Listener* (1957). She added that *Narrative of a Child Analysis* was destined to be "a very voluminous book." (Kl 29, 6 September 1957)

At the beginning of 1958, Klein devoted a long paragraph to the trouble she was having with Lagache's *Revue* over the translation of an article on symbol formation. Lagache had asked her to revise that paper, which she had written some time previously, but Klein refused to change anything.

> Since then I had a very frank exchange of views with Lagache, telling him that I did not wish to be involved in any way with his group and that my relation with him was based purely on personal friendship; I had a very understanding answer from him, in which he said that he understood that I wanted to look after my own garden.
>
> (Kl 33, 31 January 1958)

In the same letter, Klein wrote that she had refused to allow Lagache to publish in the *Revue* a chapter taken from *Contributions to Psycho-Analysis* because she did not want to have anything to do with Lagache's more recent approach. At the same time, she spoke of the difficulties she had come up against personally with the editors of the *Revue Française de Psychanalyse* concerning certain papers, the titles of which she does not mention in her letter.

> They are not well disposed towards me and my work, otherwise more than, I think, two papers of mine would have appeared in that *Revue*. On the other hand, it is possible that they do not want to show this openly. I had a good

deal of correspondence about the publication of some of my papers with Mme Bonaparte's secretary, and the excuse they gave was that they had no time to translate.

(Kl 33, 31 January 1958)

In May 1959, after an interruption that lasted several months, Klein wrote to Spira saying that she was delighted to hear that *La psychanalyse des enfants* [*The Psycho-Analysis of Children*] had been published in French. "To me it is a very great satisfaction – after all, it is the fulfilment of a dream that I have had for the past 27 years." (Kl 41, 1 May 1959)

In the same letter, in which she discussed several topics at some length, Klein wrote that she was very pleased to have received a review, published in Geneva,[12] of her book *Envy and Gratitude*. She was preparing a lecture that she was due to give at Manchester University to a group of sociologists on "Our adult world and its roots in early infancy" (Klein 1959). There she would meet several important people in university circles, a fact that gave rise to some degree of apprehension in her.

I am a bit anxious whether I shall be able to convey to a University audience, who probably know very little about psycho-analysis, my concepts, which I am not diluting but only explaining. Unfortunately, I shall not know whether they understand me, as there will be no discussion and they are very pleasant and too polite to tell me. Anyhow I shall do my best and, in the course of time, I have got so used to the idea that only part of what I say is understood that I am not too worried about it.

(Kl 41, 1 May 1959)

In her letter dated 16 January 1960, among other topics, Klein wrote that she was at that point revising her manuscript of *Narrative of a Child Analysis*. She added that she was writing something else which was still at an "infant stage" but destined to be part of a short book that would be published the following year— she did not, however, go into any more details about that project. She had just learned—with some satisfaction—that a famous American publisher was intending to print a paperback version of *The Psycho-Analysis of Children*.

If this comes off, it will be an enormous advantage, because then this book will become read widely in the United States. It will amuse you to hear that my work is referred to in the course of Psychology for students in Cleveland, Ohio, but they are warned it is not valid according to American Psycho-Analysts. This seems to have started an urge to read it among some students; they got in touch with Miss Evans, who, it seems, managed to impress them.

12 I have been unable to find any reference to this article.

I think that in twenty years, when I should certainly not be here to see it, the work of my American colleagues will be found to be invalid and my work valid. I hope that my young colleagues will have the pleasure of seeing this.

(Kl 42, 16 January 1960)

In the last letter she wrote to Spira, on 1 July 1960, Klein said that she was delighted to read that Spira had finished translating the *Contributions* book; she thought it better that Spira should wait until the following autumn before contacting Lagache with a view to finding a publisher. She hoped that Spira would have an enjoyable time in Argentina and asked her to give her best wishes to all those whom she (Klein) knew there, especially Marie Langer. Melanie Klein died in London a little over two months later, on 22 September 1960.

A Kleinian psychoanalyst in the Swiss Psychoanalytical Society

A significant part of Klein's letters to Spira deals with the difficulties that the latter was encountering in her attempts to fit in with her Swiss colleagues on her arrival in Geneva in September 1955, a few months after leaving Argentina. It is true, of course, that to some extent the suspicion and hostility encountered by Spira was linked to the fact that she declared herself to be, as I have mentioned, the representative of Melanie Klein's innovative ideas. That said, her attachment to the Kleinian way of thinking was not in itself a sufficient explanation. I think that there were other grounds—for example, her fear of not having any patients or her disappointment at not being immediately accepted as a member of the Swiss Society. In several of her letters, Klein encouraged Spira to keep on trying and, from 1959 on, Spira did indeed appear to be reassured by the importance she had in her colleagues' eyes thereafter.

Klein's encouragement

As early as the second letter that she wrote to Spira, dated 18 November 1955, Klein promised her that she would support her in dealing with the difficulties that Spira was having in her attempt to become a member of the Swiss Society; Spira had told Klein of these difficulties during their meeting and in her early letters. From Klein's answers, it would seem that Spira was surprised at not being welcomed with open arms by her colleagues as soon as she arrived in Geneva; she had apparently painted a pessimistic picture of the psychoanalytic landscape that she had discovered in Switzerland. Klein encouraged Spira to tell her straight out how she felt about the situation, promising not to repeat her comments to anyone.

"I am not surprised that they find you astonishing in Switzerland, where I believe analysis is very backward, but the courage and confidence with which you understand your task seems to augur well for success."

(Kl 2, 18 November 1955)

"Psycho-analysis in Switzerland has stagnated for many years and the influence of de Saussure does not appear perhaps to be as fruitful as one should wish, though I shall be very pleased to hear your opinion, which you can express quite firmly to me and which, if you so wish, will not be communicated to anybody else."

(Kl 3, 6 January 1956)

Klein's next letter mentioned one that Spira had sent to her, telling Klein of her worry about the situation she found herself in five months after her arrival in Geneva.

I am extremely sorry that you find yourself in such difficulties. I always thought it would be a very hard task to try to introduce into Switzerland and in particular in Geneva where now de Saussure reigns, actual psychoanalysis, but I thought that you had not only the pioneer spirit to do that, but also the means to hold out for a longer time. Though difficult, I would not have thought it an impossible thing to do, but the pre-condition would be that you could wait until patients turn up, which I believe they would do in due time.

I am fully aware of the difficulties which a pioneer has to encounter but as I said, the financial aspect is extremely important. If you could hold out a year or two you might find that you would not only get patients, but be able to change the situation.

I am very sorry that, in the circumstances, I really cannot give you any advice. It would be a great pity for your sake and for the sake of psychoanalysis (and even for Switzerland) if you have to give up what you have embarked on.

(Kl 4, 13 February, 1955)

On 16 March 1956 (Kl 5), Klein wrote to Spira to let her know that a Mrs Kate Schüftan,[13] who had been living in London for the previous few months, was interested in Kleinian psychoanalysis and would be contacting Spira in order to begin analysis once she [Mrs Schüftan] returned to Geneva. One month later, Klein wrote that she was glad to read that Spira was beginning to have patients in analysis, for that would help her face up to any difficulties, whether financial or as

13 Käthe (or Kate) Schüftan was a German-Jewish physician who became a naturalized Swiss citizen. She worked in the Münzingen Psychiatric Clinic, then in Geneva. A trainee analyst with the Swiss Psychoanalytical Society, she later settled in Israel (K. Weber, C. Müller and B. Feyer, personal communication).

far as her morale was concerned. Klein had something to say also about the character of Philip Sarasin who was at that time President of the Swiss Psychoanalytical Society.[14] Spira must have said something to Klein about Sarasin's opposing her attempts to become a member of the society, hence Klein's repeated encouragements to Spira to keep on trying.

> I was very pleased to see from your letter that your practice is growing. As I told you before, if you can hold out financially I believe that you will – Sarasin or not – make your way in Geneva. Sarasin, who is quite ossified, was already so 20 years ago and always extremely hostile to my work and to me personally, so I am afraid you will get some of that on to you, but with the optimism which I have always possessed (as well as scepticism) I believe you will find many students and people in Geneva interested in something which is good, and your pioneer work may carry more weight than whatever obstacles Sarasin is trying to put in your way. It is amazing how people gather that somebody works better than others and I think you also have the temperament to put your views forward effectively in the society, even though they may not like to hear them.
>
> You will realise that none of this is new to me. When I read my paper to the British Society "Some Schizoid Mechanisms" – and by then I had already worked 20 years in England – I found there very few people who understood it and I cannot really say I had a particular success with it. That has changed in the meantime, though I still meet with stubborn hostility on the part of the group represented by Anna Freud, but there are many signs that the time will come, sooner or later, when they will not be able to keep this up. There is no doubt that they take much more notice of me now in the United States as well.
>
> (Kl 6, 29 March 1956)

Two months later, on 3 May 1956 (Kl 7), Klein wrote to Spira saying that she was delighted to learn that, in addition to the patients Spira had by then in analysis, she was also supervising child and adult psychoanalyses. She added that once Spira was accepted as a member of the Swiss Society—no doubt in December of that same year—it would be the start of a very promising career. Klein went on to invite Spira to London in June, specifically since she wanted to discuss with her a paper that Spira was intending to read quite soon afterwards at a meeting of the Swiss Society.

---

14 Philip Sarasin became president of the Swiss Society at the end of the 1920s and remained in that post for more than thirty years.

Hanna Segal's visits to Switzerland

In a long letter that she wrote to Spira five days later, on 8 May 1956 (Kl 8), Klein answered a request that Spira had addressed to her: she had asked Klein if, in her opinion, she could invite Paula Heimann to give a lecture in Switzerland. Klein suggested that they should invite Hanna Segal rather than Paula Heimann and gave her reasons in a handwritten postscript. Klein added that she had met Raymond de Saussure during the celebrations for the centenary of Freud's birth. De Saussure had asked Klein in a very friendly way who could represent the Kleinian group at the forthcoming Lausanne meeting; he too had been thinking of Paula Heimann.

> I was not in favour of the person you suggest and whom he [de Saussure] also suggested to me (for reasons which I shall explain a little later) but I told him that I knew somebody more suitable and more capable to do it, and that is Dr. Segal, who is also the one amongst us who can speak the best French. [...] I felt very happy indeed about this development and I was delighted that Dr. Segal agreed to do this. I really think she is by far the best person both to explain my work succinctly and also not to be provocative, and de Saussure was very pleased when I told him that her way of presenting things was not provocative. I had the impression that he is quite determined to have her there, and when I remember his attitude one or two years ago it seems to me a tremendous achievement on your part. *He was really friendly and interested* [handwritten].
>
>   I am glad that my prophecy that if you could hold out in Geneva for a little while you would win through in the end seems to have come true, but that does not alter my very great appreciation of what you have done and are doing. It will, though, be a much better proposition that somebody from London, and who is used to representing this work, should speak on this occasion instead of your undertaking a task which seems to me really too heavy in the present state of affairs.
>
> (Kl 8, 8 May 1956)

Klein added that it would be advisable for Spira to be careful during the discussions and to avoid challenging René Spitz or Serge Lebovici directly; it would be better to leave that sort of thing to Hanna Segal, who knew them well. "All this may not really have to do with you, because if you contribute in the discussion I think you will probably just speak of your experience, and that seems to me by far the wisest course to take." (Kl 8, 8 May 1956)

   Klein went on to say that the centenary celebrations passed off very well. Ernest Jones, who had just returned from a lecture tour in the United States, gave an excellent talk on "The nature of greatness": "There are some people who use these occasions for self-advertisement; but he [Jones] is not one of them, but I am glad he got the tributes he so richly deserves."

This is how that letter ends:

> I was delighted about Dr. de Saussure's invitation to Dr. Segal and also about her being so willing to accept it; the whole thing is the best news I have had for some time and your part in it is fully appreciated by me and by my friends (…)
>
> With love, yours,
>
> Melanie Klein.
>
> (Kl 8, 8 May 1956)

In a handwritten postscript, Klein told Spira that Paula Heimann had left the Kleinian group.

> Dr. Heimann is no longer a member of my group. This is well known in England since she made it public that she is now a member of the Independent Group (formerly called Middle Group) but this fact is not known abroad. This piece of news will come as a surprise and shock to you, but it was, though very painful, not a great surprise to me. I have seen it coming for years. This is too complex and painful to go into any details about it, but I feel you should know the fact. All my other friends and colleagues stand firmly by me.
>
> (Kl 8, 8 May 1956)

A few days after the Lausanne meeting, Klein wrote to Spira to say that she was delighted to hear, from Hanna Segal, that the meeting had been a success.

> The success she had was based on the work you have done during the year and I cannot thank you enough for what you are doing. It must also be a great satisfaction to you to have succeeded so well in one year in what seemed to begin with an extremely difficult venture.
>
> (Kl 9, 31 July 1956)

Gradually becoming less and less isolated

During the following seven months, Klein's and Spira's letters have mainly to do with various issues concerning the translation of the footnotes to the French edition of *The Psycho-Analysis of Children*, a task that Spira had undertaken at Klein's request. No more was said about Spira's earlier difficulties with respect to finding her place within the Swiss Psychoanalytical Society. Those issues did, however, come to the fore again; in her letter dated 22 February 1957 (Kl 19), Klein discussed the steps Spira had taken with a view to becoming a member of the Swiss Society, the outcome of her application being somewhat uncertain:

I was very sorry to hear that your situation is not easy, but actually I never expected it to be and since, as I hope, your time is still occupied, I think you can leave further solutions to time. It would, of course, be very nice if you receive your Membership, but if you do not get it I do not think it will prevent people from appreciating your work. I am telling you this from experience, though of course when I came to England I had Dr. Jones' very strong support, but nevertheless I have come fully to the conviction that good work wins in the end. I am now getting from all sorts of places in the United States signs of interest and expressions of the wish to learn, and this is from people who have no direct contact with me as the Swiss now have with you.

(Kl 19, 22 February 1957)

In April 1957, however, Klein was able to congratulate Spira on becoming a member of the Swiss Psychoanalytical Society, adding that she was sure that the paper that Spira would be presenting would be well received. The subject of Spira's paper had to do with literature; Klein wrote that she did not feel qualified to say anything about that topic, because it was one that she had neglected somewhat, being too busy with her own writing (Kl 22, 5 April 1957).

Eight months later, on 10 January 1958 (Kl 32), Klein wrote to Spira asking how her paper was progressing—Spira had over the months made no further mention of it—and when she was thinking of presenting it.

It is good news that in spite of the difficulties which are no doubt increased through the French child analysts, you are not losing courage. I have come to the conclusion that all these personal matters and difficulties, of which we have also plenty in this Society here, are not important and can be counteracted by good books appearing. My book is getting on and I [learned that] "Envy and Gratitude" is selling very well, and there are two or [three other] books in preparation, by Dr. Segal, Dr. Bion and also [I presume], by Dr. Rosenfeld. Your personal influence, your knowledge and [your] determination should also carry great weight. I am glad to see [that you] share my feeling that nothing, in the long run, is going to [prevent the] truth. After many years of difficulties, I have not lost [confidence] and I am happy to find that my younger colleagues [develop the same] attitude.

(Kl 32, 10 January 1958)

Three weeks later, Klein again stressed how important it was for Spira to finish writing her paper, a major text that Spira kept on revising. "I am glad that you take so much trouble over it, and re-read and reformulate, because I know from my own experience that that will very likely improve the paper. (Kl 33, 31 January 1958)

On 13 June 1958, Klein had no difficulty in finding the right words for sympathizing with Spira's feeling of isolation; she wrote at some length of her own isolation both at that time and in the past:

I am sorry to hear that your position among your Swiss colleagues is still so difficult and I am fully in sympathy with the isolation in which you are as far as work is concerned, but I am not in the least surprised. Your undertaking to introduce real analysis into Switzerland is such a difficult and important pioneer work that it would be surprising if it were easier than it has turned out to be. I wish you had one or two colleagues who would join you in Switzerland. [...] It is very difficult to stand by oneself, and it needs a great deal of courage and strength, but I believe you have these two qualities and therefore I do not doubt that in the end you will come through. The great thing is that you have patience. I myself have experienced so much isolation that I can fully sympathise with your position. Even now, when I have a number of capable and reliable colleagues to share my work, the feeling of isolation has by no means gone. In a Society where I have worked for 32 years, I can still find a striking lack of understanding and goodwill in the majority of colleagues. My answer to their lack of interest, to their envy and jealousy, was always to write and, as it happens, in spite of the controversial position in which I still am, there is no doubt that my work is making its way. Again and again I get confirmation of this. Jones used to tell me 'The truth must come through', but truth has the quality of being inconvenient, therefore one has to be resigned to the fact that it is always only a minority that can accept it. However, this minority is of great importance.

(Kl 35, 13 June 1958)

Three months later, Klein wrote some more words of encouragement to Spira.

[I]t may turn out that you will, by and by, find a number of new people who will co-operate with you, which will change the character of the Swiss Society. You may think that I am too optimistic, but actually I have gone through similar experiences myself and, in spite of everything to the contrary, good work does attract some people and those it attracts are usually good.

(Kl 38, 26 September 1958)

The encouragements that Klein sent Spira appeared to bear fruit: in a later handwritten message, Klein said that she was very pleased to learn that Spira was having considerable success in her work.

It always gladdens my heart to know of success by one of my friends and collaborators and by success I don't only mean external prestige, but good work done, conviction and also expression of the work done by writing. Are there among your analysands also future Swiss analysts?

(Kl 40, 18 December 1958)

Just over a year went by without Klein saying anything more about Spira's situation within the Swiss Society. Her letters had to do with other matters. It would seem likely, therefore, that throughout 1959 Spira's position in Geneva and in Switzerland as a whole had gradually improved. The letter that Klein sent to her in January 1960 would appear to confirm that impression.

> I was very glad to hear from you after this long silence, but the important thing is that the news you give me is good, both as far as you personally are concerned, and the work that you are doing. [...] I have in the course of forty years, learned not to become indifferent towards misrepresentation or hostility, but to consider that, in spite of all, there is constant progress going on. Believe me, I highly value your efforts, and it gives me great pleasure to hear that the strength you put in your purpose is not diminished.
>
> (Kl 42, 16 January 1960)

In her three final letters, Klein made no mention of any difficulties that Spira might have been encountering as regards the Swiss Psychoanalytical Society, so that it would seem logical to conclude that, by then, Spira had managed to find her rightful place among her colleagues.

A little family news

Klein's letters and those that we can suppose that Spira wrote to her hardly ever mention their respective families or relatives. When some mention is made, both the first name and the surname of the person concerned are not divulged. In Klein's twenty-third letter, she mentioned the fortnight that she had spent in Holland with her grandson during the Easter holiday, saying that she had had a very happy time (Kl 23, 9 May 1957). In a letter dated 19 December 1957 (Kl 31), Klein congratulated Spira on her son's forthcoming marriage[15] and, in a subsequent letter, she asked Spira to send him and his wife her best wishes (Kl 32, 10 January 1958).

That gave Klein the opportunity to say a few words about how happy she felt at being a grandmother.

> Since you are looking forward to grandchildren, I hope this will come true in due time. I myself derive my greatest pleasure from my grandchildren – satisfaction about work is of a quite different nature, and has a good deal to do also with feelings of duty, that I have to do my best to keep this work alive.
>
> (Kl 31, 19 December 1957)

On 26 September 1958 (Kl 38), Klein said that she was sorry to hear that Spira's mother had had an accident (a fall?) which had given rise to complications. Three months later, in a handwritten letter, Klein sent her condolences to Spira, whose mother had just died. That event reminded Klein of how she had felt when her own mother had died.

---

15 Gilbert Schwob; there is no mention either of his surname or of his first name in the letter.

My mother's death caused me great pain and it took me some time to get over the depression which followed. How often do I think about her even now and miss her – in some way she remains alive with me! So I know what you have gone through and my thoughts are with you. I did not realise that your mother had been so ill and therefore did not connect your silence with all the trouble and anxiety you have gone through.

(Kl 40, 18 December 1958)

There is another brief piece of family news in the letter that Klein wrote on 1 May 1959 (Kl 41), in which she told Spira of her plans for the summer. She hoped to meet Spira in Copenhagen at the IPA Congress; from there she would travel to Gothenburg to visit her sister-in-law and then head for Switzerland, where she would spend her summer holiday in Wengen. In her penultimate letter, dated 25 March 1960 (Kl 44), Klein told Spira that she was glad that her family had insisted that her grandson accompany her so that she would not be travelling alone. In fact, as I have written earlier, both her son Eric and her grandson Michael went with her.

Klein's failing health

From time to time, Klein briefly mentioned her health in some of the letters she wrote, although generally speaking she remained very discreet on the subject right up to the end. On 18 November 1955 (Kl 2), this is what she wrote to Spira:

I am keeping well, but the pre-condition is that I do not do too much work and have sufficient rest. This of course slows down my writing (not to speak of my correspondence) which I can only do on some mornings because in the evenings I am not able to do it. The time is past when I wrote my 'Psycho-Analysis of Children' and most of the papers you are translating in evenings or over weekends.

(Kl 2, 18 November 1955)

Giving news of her health was a more common occurrence in the letters she wrote to Spira during the last two years of her life, although here again she wrote only briefly about the topic and in a way that could hardly have given rise to any alarm. On 17 August 1958, she sent a handwritten note to Spira from the Sandridge Park Hotel in Melksham, where she was spending the summer holiday. She again said that the previous winter had been a difficult time for her because she had been asked to do so many things. "[…] and altogether I did not feel too well. Nothing serious. But a desire to be able to use my remaining strength in the best and most gratifying way – a wish not easily fulfilled." (Kl 36, 18 August 1958)

In the only letter we have that was written in 1959, Klein said that she regretted the fact that she would not have enough time to finish the paper she was due to read in Manchester University. "Though I do not think that my mental capacity has deteriorated in quality, it has certainly slowed up in recent years. However, I hope to finish next week […].” (Kl 41, 1 May 1959)

In March 1960, Klein told Spira that she was planning to spend her summer holiday in Villars-sur-Ollon, in Switzerland, and mentioned that she was feeling tired. In two letters that she wrote in a short space of time, she again spoke of her state of health.

> I am tired but not unwell and it seems that Villars will be a good place for a good holiday – very much needed.
>
> (Kl 43, 17 March 1960)

> I am very glad that the winter is over. Although I did not have a single cold, I did not feel well, and there were quite a lot of factors contributing to this. I am glad the spring is coming. I think that my power of recuperation is still there.
>
> (Kl 44, 25 March 1960)

The last letter that Klein wrote to Spira, dated 1 July 1960, ends as follows: “I am writing in a hurry, so I shall only say that I am keeping fairly well, though of course at times I get tired, which is not surprising at my age.” (Kl 45, 1 July 1960)

There is nothing in that letter to suggest that less than three months later, on 22 September 1960, Klein would be dead. She was 78 years of age.

A self-portrait by Klein in her final years

Melanie Klein’s letters to Marcelle Spira are not only historical documents full of interesting information about various aspects of Klein’s life, they also throw light on the friendship that grew up between the two women in the period between their first meeting in 1955 and Klein’s death in 1960. That first meeting was purely professional, in the sense that Spira took the opportunity of discussing with Klein certain issues of a scientific nature. However, rather than staying simply with an exchange of letters, Klein immediately suggested that Spira come to London so that they could continue their discussion and bring in some of Klein’s followers to share in it. Over and beyond their scientific dialogue, Klein’s warmth indicated that she wanted a less formal relationship with Spira, one that would be less marked by idealization. Spira’s short stay in London brought them closer together and transformed their relationship from one that could have remained similar to that between student and teacher to one that was much more personal, with mutual trust and respect. From that point on, Klein no longer prefaced her letters with “Dear Madame Spira” but with “Dear Marcelle”.

Without going into any detail as regards this exchange of letters between Klein and Spira, we could ask ourselves what cemented their relationship? It is important to note the context in which Spira was writing to Klein at that time. For political reasons, Spira had had to leave Argentina, where she had worked for many years.

She arrived in Switzerland in a professional environment which was completely foreign to her and which was not particularly willing to welcome a new approach to psychoanalysis. In my opinion, the decisive element was the fact that, in Klein, Spira found someone with whom she could discuss matters in complete confidentiality. Spira shared with Klein the distress and loneliness she felt when faced with the lack of understanding of her fellow psychoanalysts; and Klein was all the more able to understand Spira, to be attentive to her distress and to tell her that things would turn out all right because she too had been in a similar difficult situation and had managed to break free of it thanks to her force of character and perseverance.

Last but not least, reading between the lines of these letters provides us with a self-portrait painted by Melanie Klein over the last five years of her life. That aspect, to my mind, is the most important element that this hitherto unpublished exchange of letters offers us. I shall leave it up to the reader to make that discovery for him- or herself.

Chapter 5

Transcription of the 45 letters that Melanie Klein sent to Marcelle Spira[16]

Preliminary explanations	
Kl 25, 1-3	Number of the original letter and pages
//	Page break in the original (two oblique lines in the text)
Chère Marcelle (regular font)	Typewritten text
Chère Marcelle (italic font)	Handwritten text
[t] (regular font)	Letter or word added by Klein and suppressed by the author (e.g. "…includes this point though[t] it will be much more developed…")
[*t*] (italic font)	Letter or word corrected or added by the author (e.g. "It would be a great pity for you[*r*] sake…")
Words or phrases <u>underlined</u>	Underlined in the original

The original order of words has been followed, even if at times it does not quite correspond to ordinary British English syntax (e.g. "You used it already", where in British English one would tend to say "You already used it").

---

16 The original correspondence has been deposited as a loan with the Melanie Klein Trust in London.

Kl 1

20, Bracknell Gardens
London N.W.3

21 October 1955

Dear Madame Spira,

I hope that my letter will find you at your actual address since I have been given one by Madame Pichon-Rivière[17] and another (in Neuchatel) by Professor Lagache[18], but I assume that the one Madame Pichon-Rivière gave me is the latest.

As you may imagine I am deeply interested in your very kind intention to translate my "Contributions"[19]. I do not know when you will start on them but I should be glad, when you have translated one of the papers, to see it. I have no doubt that, like my other translators, you would wish me to see something of the translation before you complete the work and to discuss with you certain points which might arise.

I much enjoyed meeting you at the Congress and am sorry there was no more opportunity for a really good talk with you, but there never is at any Congress. Perhaps you will come to London some time and that would be a better opportunity.

I hope that you have settled down to your satisfaction and I have no doubt that you have much scope for work in your country.

Yours Sincerely,

Melanie Klein

---

17 Arminda Aberastury (1910–1972), an Argentinian psychoanalyst, married Enrique Pichon-Rivière in 1937. She translated into Spanish *The Psycho-Analysis of Children*.
18 Daniel Lagache (1903–1972) was a French psychoanalyst. In 1938, he was the first to deliver lectures on psychoanalysis in a French university. He was Professor of Psychology and Psychopathology in the Sorbonne, and a co-founder of the French Psychoanalytical Association in 1964.
19 Klein, M. (1948).

Kl 2, 1-3

20, Bracknell Gardens
London N.W.3

18 November 1955

Chère Madame Spira,

Many thanks for your kind letter. I am of course delighted to hear that the translation is progressing but should be very glad to see one chapter. I am fully aware that revisions will be necessary when the translation is more advanced, but in the meantime I might have some suggestions to make which would be helpful during the process of translation.

I am keeping well, but the pre-condition is that I do not do too much work and have sufficient rest. This of course slows down my writing (not to speak of my correspondence) which I can only do on some mornings because in the evenings I am not able to do it. The time is past when I wrote my "Psycho-Analysis of Children" and most of the Papers you are translating on evenings or over weekends. This is the reason why I have only recently read your Congress Paper[20].

I found this Paper very interesting and it shows that you are doing good work and have original thoughts. I was also gratified to find that you seemed to have very well understood my concepts. If there is anything I would suggest, it is that it might be helpful if you described the paranoid-schizoid position (to which you refer) in a similar way as you defined the depressive position because some of the conclusions you draw as regards memory I would also consider from the angle of the splitting processes in the first few months of life. The importance of projective identification in the patient you describe seems to me very great and it might be worthwhile to connect your conclusions with this concept as well. On the whole, I enjoyed your Paper very much and was pleased to meet a colleague who could look so deeply.

I am not surprised that they find you astonishing in Switzerland, where I believe analysis is very backward, // but the courage and confidence with which you undertake your task seems to augur well for success.

It would be a great pleasure if you came to London and we could then have some talks for which the Congress unfortunately did not allow. I shall certainly be very pleased to make any suggestions which would be helpful for the translation, but there are more and general points which I should be glad to have an opportunity to talk over with you, which are not so easy for me to discuss by correspondence.

However, I shall answer your questions about the epileptic child as well as I can[21]. I think this case, though no doubt very instructive from a general point of view, is

---

20 Spira, M. (1959).
21 Spira, M. (1966). See also Eissler, R. S. (1954).

of a specific nature. As you yourself stress, there is the perseveration of the epileptic and that may account for the long period which passed until the effects of the analysis showed. I would agree with your suggestion that arrested development implies very slow elaboration. If it is a question of regression, the fact that stages have already been reached in the past makes for a much quicker result. Nevertheless, it is true that even more normal children also need some length of time until they can work through unconsciously the insight they are gaining, but the word "working through" is the clue, I think, for this. The same applies to adults. We have again and again to "work through" material until stabilisation is achieved. You know how much Freud thought of "working through" as a part of the analytic procedure and I am more than ever convinced that that is a most essential factor.

I need not elaborate on the reasons why the working through is a pre-condition for successful analysis, because I am sure you have observed that again and again defences against insight bound up with anxiety arise. It is my belief that the analysis has to take enough time and there is no prospect whatever, in my view, even if our technique improves, of shortening it.

We even have to allow that patients after having finished the analysis, still need a certain period for settling down, which I think is part of the mourning process // about finishing the analysis. I have referred to this in my paper on the Termination of an Analysis.

Thank you again for the interest you show in my work and for the great trouble you are taking in translating it, which I realise is a very hard task.

With my best wishes,

Yours

Melanie Klein

Kl 3, 1-2

20, Bracknell Gardens
London N.W.3

6 January 1956

Chère Madame Spira,

I apologise for the delay in replying to your letter, but I am quite sure you will forgive me for that.

I was extremely interested in what you said about the regressions necessarily taking place in artists: this corresponds to a large extent with my own views. I wonder whether you know Dr. Segal's paper "A Psycho-Analytical Approach to Aesthetics" [Segal, 1952], which has already appeared in the Birthday Number – and that reminds me that at last the book containing 21 contributions, being an enlarged version of the Birthday Number, has come out under the title "New Directions in Psycho-Analysis" (published by Tavistock Publications Ltd., 2 Beaumont Street, London, W.1).

To return to the point I made in my last letter – the fundamental importance of the paranoid-schizoid position which I have recently linked with excessive envy. It is in this position that the basis for insanity lies, and so much depends on how far it can be modified in the course of development or of analysis. In the book which I am now writing, the enlarged version of my Congress Paper, I make a particular point that excessive envy indicates particularly strong schizoid and paranoid trends. Since it will still take quite some time before this enlarged version of my Paper will appear, I am sending you a copy of my Congress Paper[22], which also includes this point though[t] it will be much more developed in the present book. I should be glad to have this Paper back when you have read it again.

Now to the translation. I have not yet gone through it, since I assume there is no particular hurry and I was deeply engrossed in getting on with my book, but I hope within the next few weeks to go through this translation and put to you any suggestions I may have // to make. I am very willing to enter into any discussion about such points and you need not think that you have to restrain yourself in that matter. It is difficult to explain how much I have at heart the translation into French of my books, and it might give you an idea when I say that since 1932, I have aimed at getting my books well translated into French, which seems to me so important and I am very happy to think that these plans are now on the way to being realised.

You need not think of me as not being well, because I am really quite well, but it is a fact that I get much more easily tired than I used to do in the past, but even

---

22 Delivered in 1955 at the IPA Congress in Geneva under the title "A study on envy and gratitude". She would later develop the points raised in that paper and publish it in 1957 in book form: *Envy and Gratitude* (London: Tavistock Publications).

now there are many responsibilities and demands made on me, but the translation of the book is one of those demands which I have at heart and which will have priority.

I shall be very interested to hear how you are settling down in Geneva and getting on with de Saussure, who I hear [h]as very special views on psycho-analysis.

I am always pleased to receive letters from you and I know that you will not expect me to answer them promptly. Psycho-analysis in Switzerland has stagnated for many years and the influence of de Saussure does not appear perhaps to be as fruitful as one would wish. I shall be very pleased to hear your opinions which you can express quite firmly to me and which, if you so wish, will not be communicated to anybody else.

With Kindest regards,

Yours,

Melanie Klein

Kl 4, 1-2

20, Bracknell Gardens
London N.W.3

13 February 1956

Chère Madame Spira,

Thank you very much for your letter. First of all I wish to say that I am extremely sorry that you find yourself in such difficulties. I always thought it would be a very hard task to try to introduce into Switzerland and in particular Geneva where now de Saussure reigns, actual psycho-analysis, but I thought that you had not only the pioneer spirit to do that, but also the means to hold out for a longer time. Though difficult, I would not have thought it an impossible thing to do, but the pre-condition would be that you could wait until patients turn up, which I believe they would do in time.

I am fully aware of the difficulties which a pioneer has to encounter but as I said, the financial aspect is extremely important. If you could hold out a year or two you might find that you would not only get patients, but be able to change the situation.

I am very sorry that, in the circumstances, I really cannot give you any advice. It would be a great pity for you[r] sake and for the sake of psycho-analysis (and even for Switzerland) if you had to give up what you have embarked on.

The other contents of your letter I found, as usual, very interesting but am at the moment not able to reply in detail. I shall send you in time the enlarged version of my Congress Paper which I read a week ago to the British Society. Since as I have told you I am working out the whole thing into a small book, this is only a provisional version but contains much more than my Congress Paper and therefore in the meantime [m]ight be of interest to you.

The formulation of my paper on Symbol Formation[23] which you refer to, I would certainly now present quite differently. It was only one of those steps, and not an unimportant one, which leads one to further progress. //

In the meantime, my best wishes, and please let me know how things are going with you. I am keeping fairly well, though the cold weather does not at all agree with me.

Yours ever,

Melanie Klein

P.S. Thank you for returning the Congress Paper.

23 Klein, M. (1930).

Kl 5

20, Bracknell Gardens
London N.W.3

16 March 1956

Chère Madame Spira,

At last I have been able to go more thoroughly through your translation of the chapters you sent me and I am very pleased with it. There will of course be, as usual, a few points to be discussed but I gather from your letter that you would be quite willing to my making suggestions. I must apologise for having delayed going through these chapters for so long and I hope it has not put you off from going on with it, but this winter was not a very good one for me. I was not ill but felt tired: the cold did not agree with me and the best I could do was to go on with my work and continue with the book on Envy and Gratitude which I have so much at heart. Everything else – correspondence, translations, etc. – suffered under this fact, but I know very well that you are understanding and will forgive me for the long delay in giving you my *good* opinion on the translation.

I am extremely interested in how you find the situation in Geneva and if there is any improvement since you wrote to me.

There is a woman analyst, Dr. Schüftan[24], who has been staying in London for some months, and who is very interested in my work, who intends to be analysed by you since it was impossible for her to stay long enough in England to be analysed here. I wonder whether she has been in touch with you? Her intention was to work in Lausanne where she has connections, and to go to you for analysis. This at least was her plan.

I shall be glad to hear from you.

Yours *with best wishes*

Melanie Klein

---

24 See footnote 13, p. 34.

Kl 6, 1-3

20, Bracknell Gardens
London N.W.3

29 March 1956

Chère Madame Spira,

I was very pleased to see from your letter that your practice is growing. As I told you before, if you can hold out financially I believe that you will, Sar[a]sin[25] or not, make your way in Geneva. Sarasin, who is quite ossified, was already so 20 years ago and always extremely hostile to my work and to me personally, so I am afraid you will get some of that on to you, but with the optimism which I have always possessed (as well as scepticism) I believe you will find many students and people in Geneva interested in something which is good, and your pioneer work may carry more weight than whatever obstacles Sarasin is trying to put in your way. It is amazing how people gather that somebody works better than others and I think you also have the temperament to put your views forward effectively in the Society, even though they may not like to hear them.

You will realise that none of this is new to me. When I read my paper to the British Society "Some Schizoid Mechanisms"[26] – and by then I had already worked 20 years in England – I found there were very few people who understood it and I cannot really say I had any particular success with it. That has changed in the meantime, though I still meet with stubborn hostility on the part of the group represented by Anna Freud[27], but there are many signs that the time will come, sooner or later, when they will not be able to keep this up. There is no doubt that they take much more notice of me now in the United States as well.

I am sending you a copy of a review which appeared in the Times Literary Supplement which is, on the whole, very friendly. I must explain that a review in this Journal is thought by Literary people to come next in importance to the Bible, and the importance of such a review can be gathered by the fact that Dr. Jones[28] explained to me, when I first came to England, that should I get a review in the Supplement, one should not mind unfavourable comment but measure it in inches. //

I was extremely pleased with it and so were my friends. It is also a piece of good news for us that the American publishers, Basic Books Inc., want to print New Directions themselves and will make the first edition of 5000 copies.

Now to your translation.

I shall not be able, chère Madame Spira, to give you details about where I think some alterations might be advisable before the autumn, but this should not hold up your translation, if you find time for it, because my suggestions are not of a general

---

25 Philip Sarasin (1888–1968), from Basle, became president of the Swiss Psychoanalytical Society in 1928 and remained at that post for 32 years, until Raymond de Saussure succeeded him in 1960.
26 Klein, M. (1946).
27 Anna Freud (1895–1982), Sigmund Freud's daughter.
28 Ernest Jones (1879–1958), the British psychoanalyst, helped Klein to come to England in 1926.

nature. It is only very occasionally that I think something might be put differently and therefore it does not apply to the translation as a whole.

Thank you very much for letting me know about Baranger, who I have been told is a very good translator and has been helping, I think, in the translation of my "Contributions" into Spanish. I have mentioned his willingness to translate the "New Directions" to Lagache but I am very doubtful whether at the moment I should really ask him (I have got his address) for this translation *for the following reason.*

The translation of the "Psycho-Analysis of Children" has been stuck ever[y] since Madame Boulanger died and though Dr. Boulanger has the best intentions and promises me from time to time that he will continue it, it is now in the 5th year since the translation was started and ever since his wife's unfortunate death he has not continued the translation. Whether he will go on with it or not I shall see within the next few months. If he cannot – because I am sure he has got the best intentions – then I shall ask him to give up and might then turn to Baranger for a continuation of this translation. I still believe that the main book to be translated into French would be "The Psycho-Analysis of Children", however much I would be pleased with the translation of later books.

Professor Servadio[29] of Rome plans now the translation of some analytic books and since he obviously has in mind only a smaller book by me I have suggested to him the translation of my latest one. *This* I hope will go to the *English and American* publishers before the summer holidays (that is one of the reasons why I have no time at present to make my suggestions about your translation). So the prospects seem quite bright at the moment. //

As regards *Dr. Schüftan*, she has decided in the meantime to stay another term in England because she feels she is now beginning more to understand my work and that of my colleagues. I am not sure whether she will in fact approach you for an analysis, but I must warn you that though she is extremely interested in my work, she knows very little about it, only what she gathered from lectures and seminars during the last few months of her stay in London. I cannot believe that she will get much further without an analysis, since her first one I think was not of great value.

I am telling you this because you should not expect too much of the collaboration with somebody who, though having interest and good intentions, knows in fact little. It is possible, though, that she might decide to be analysed by you and that is the best thing she could do.

I feel much better since the weather has improved and I am just about to go away for a fortnight's holiday in the country.

I hope you will have had a pleasurable Easter holiday.

With Kindest Regards,

Yours ever

Melanie Klein

---

29 Emilio Servadio (1904–1995) was one of the founder members of the Italian Psychoanalytical Society in 1932.

Kl 6, attachment

THE TIMES LITERARY SUPPLEMENT FRIDAY MARCH 23 1956

EXPLORING THE CHILD MIND

MELANIE KLEIN, PAULA HEIMANN AND R.E. MONEY-KRYLE (Editors):

New Directions in Psycho-Analysis   Tavistock Publications 38s

The origin of psycho-analysis was, of course, Freud's discovery of the method of "free association" in the treatment of adults suffering from various forms of neurosis. As everyone knows, his results led to a radically new conception of the child's mind and of the part played by early experiences in the development of neurotic illness. Freud did not, however, himself work with children to any extent and it was largely left to others to test the validity of his theories against direct observations of children's behaviour. Among these, the most distinguished – as well as the most original – has undoubtedly been Mrs. Melanie Klein, for whom the present volume is something in the nature of a *Festschrift*. It will be warmly welcomed by all who have gained from her influence and teaching, and by many others besides.

Beginning her work as a pupil of Karl Abraham in Berlin, Mrs. Klein quickly turned from orthodox analysis to the direct study of emotional disorders in children, basing her interpretations more especially on systematic observations of their play. Although the results of her work appeared to confirm Freud's theories at many points, divergences soon arose which led her to take a fresh standpoint towards a number of cardinal issues in Freudian theory. Thus arose what is sometimes called the "Kleinian School" of psycho-analysis, associated especially with London, where Mrs. Klein has for many years made her home. Here her ideas have caused much fluttering in the Freudian dovecotes, though they do not appear to have provoked her expulsion from the flock – a consequence, perhaps, of the more tolerant climate of London as compared with that of Vienna. One may also surmise that the doyen of British psycho-analysis, the wise and scholarly Dr. Ernest Jones (who himself contributes an appreciative foreword to this volume), has qualities of the kind so often attributed to Lord Attlee.

The most important of the "new directions" promised us is, of course, Mrs. Melanie Klein's own work on mental life in early childhood and its implications for psychological theory. The background of this work is well described by Mrs. Klein herself in the first of the two papers which she contributes to this volume. Here she reviews with verve and clarity the development of her play technique and the observations which caused her to deviate from Freud's position. It becomes clear that the findings of "play therapy" have led her to place the utmost stress upon the young child's relation to objects in the world around him and to urge that it is "object-relations" rather than "instincts" that are the critical factors in emotional development. For instance, the young child may experience both gratification and frustration with regard to the mother's breast and this may occasion a kind of split in his mind between the "good" and "bad" aspects of his relationship to it. Schisms of this kind, which arise from contradictory attitudes entertained towards one and the same object, are held to occasion emotional reactions of great importance in childhood and after. It is even suggested that they may lie at the roots of severe psychotic disorders in later life. Mrs. Klein further claims to have detected the operation of a self-punitive function – or "super-ego" – at an age much earlier than that conceived by Freud and necessitating some considerable change in his theory.

Mrs. Klein's ideas are admittedly speculative and it is difficult to see how they can very well be put to any kind of empirical test. Like Freud's system, Kleinian theory is allegorical rather than scientific, but this does not necessarily mean that it is lacking in heuristic value. Indeed several of the clinical essays assembled in this volume may be held to provide it with real, if provisional, justification. Theory apart, moreover, it can be said with confidence that Mrs. Klein's play-technique has won an assured place in the treatment of behaviour disorders in young children.

When we turn from the study of children to that of adults, Mrs. Klein and her followers might appear to be standing on more treacherous ground. Nearly half the clinical papers in this volume are concerned with problems of actual or borderline psychosis, and it is suggested that the principles derived from child study are directly applicable to their elucidation. Although psychological factors no doubt enter into every kind of mental disorder, it appears extremely improbable that its more severe forms can be ascribed in any important sense to maladjustment in early infancy. If this be conceded, it follows that the use of psycho-therapy in the treatment of the psychoses is unlikely to be attended by conspicuous benefit. (It has indeed been wholly abandoned by orthodox psychiatrists.) One may comment, therefore, that the analyses of psychotic illness presented by certain contributors to this volume may prove very misleading to the general reader. Although such analysis may provide valuable insight into the history and relationship of the mental symptoms it can discover neither cause nor cure.

The following extract does not appear in the copy addressed to Marcelle Spira:

[The wider impact of Mrs. Klein's work is well brought out in some of the papers on "applied psychoanalysis" which form the second part of this volume. Some are concerned with literary and artistic matters; others – and these are by far the most important – with tentative applications of psychoanalytical principles to the behaviour of social groups. It is not too much to say that their authors are attempting to lay the foundations of a post-Freudian social psychology.

This book is well produced and its price not excessive by present-day standards. It testifies to the existence of fresh thinking and genuine willingness to experiment with ideas on the part of psycho-analysts, and thus gives most welcome hope that the Freudian movement will not ossify into sectarian and dates dogmas. As a tribute to the indefatigable Mrs. Klein the book will be received with approval and pleasure. The editors are to be congratulated on their achievement.]

Kl 7, 1-2

20, Bracknell Gardens
London N.W.3

3 May 1956

Chère Madame Spira,

Your letter brought me very good news indeed. I was delighted to hear that my hope that you would get patients has been realised, and I am particularly pleased that you also have child cases and adult cases for supervision. I have no doubt that when you present your paper[30] in December next and are accepted officially as a member of the Swiss Association, that will be the beginning of a very fruitful career in Switzerland. I need not tell you how delighted I am that the Swiss are at last going to learn analysis, and my own experience has shown me that one person who has the perseverance, the capacity and personality to stand up can produce the most far-reaching effect.

It is an excellent opportunity, of course, that you have been asked to give lectures at that special meeting in the last week of July. I think that your choice of topics is excellent but I am quite aware how much work it involves. I fully appreciate that you would like to discuss, with me and one or two of my friends, details of these lectures, but unfortunately the first week in July is not possible for me. I have invited a sister-in-law[31], who has for many years been captive in Hungary and has at last been allowed to join her son in Sweden, to stay with me in the first part of July and I cannot alter this because she is combining it with a visit to Paris and because I myself am leaving London at the end of July. Therefore July is out of the question for me. I wonder whether you could come to London in June? I would try to keep as much time as I can. How would it be if you came to London, let us say, on the 6th June, which is a Wednesday and included the weekend or, if that is too early for you, because I realise that you are probably writing your lectures until then, one of the following weeks finishing on the 26th June? I know that might interfere with your practice, // probably you are starting your holidays in July, but I can suggest no other possibility and I agree with you that your feelings of responsibility and anxiety, which are most natural, would be diminished if you had the opportunity to discuss your plans with me and some others.

If it is possible to let me know as soon as you can make a decision I should be glad, because I would reserve as much time as I can on those days you will be in London.

I am feeling much better. My book[32] is advancing but until I have really got it at the publishers I shall not feel relieved from that burden. At the same time, I do not feel dissatisfied with this book, which could be vastly expanded if I put in more of my experiences but I feel for the purpose I wanted it is probably better to leave it as it is. In any case, I have other plans which I have to balance against one another.

Yours Ever

Melanie Klein

---

30 Spira's membership paper on memory and time.
31 Jolan, the sister of Klein's husband Arthur.
32 Klein, M. (1957).

Kl 8, 1-4

20, Bracknell Gardens
London N.W.3

8 May 1956

Chère Madame Spira,

I had written to you in reply to your letter of the 23rd April but on the same day your second letter arrived and therefore I did not post it. *I enclose my first letter.*

First of all I wish to say that I entirely agree with your decision not to give those difficult lectures in the first year of your arrival in Switzerland. You seem in any case to have worked a miracle by establishing yourself as well as you have done and you have every reason to be proud of that. I am sure it has to do with your impressing people with your work but, if I may say so, I am sure it has also to do with your personality.

In the meantime we have had the Freud Centenary celebrations[33], and de Saussure, who was very friendly, approached me straight away and asked who could attend that special meeting in Lausanne to represent my group. I was not in favour of the person you suggest and whom he also suggested to me (for reasons which I shall explain a little later) but I told him that I know somebody more suitable and more capable to do this, and that is Dr. Segal[34], who is also the one amongst us who can speak the best French. I introduced them to each other on the occasion of the fixing of the plaque at Miss Freud's reception and they seem to have agreed that she will undertake to be in Lausanne from the 23rd–27th July, but she expects to hear from him about this in writing.

I feel very happy indeed about this development and I was delighted that Dr. Segal agreed to do it. I really think she is by far the best person both to explain my work succinctly and also not to be provocative, and de Saussure was very pleased when I told him that her way of presenting things was not provocative. //

My impression is that he is quite determined to have her there, and when I remember his attitude one or two years ago it seems to me a tremendous achievement on your part. *He was really friendly and interested.*

I am glad that my prophecy that if you could hold out in Geneva for a little while you would win through in the end seems to have come true, but that does not alter my very great appreciation of what you have done and are doing. It will, though, be a much better proposition that somebody from London, and who is used to representing this work, should speak on this occasion instead of your undertaking a task which seems to me really too heavy in the present state of affairs.

---

33 On 6 May 1956, at 20 Maresfield Gardens in London. Ernest Jones unveiled a plaque in memory of Freud.

34 Hanna Segal (1918–2011).

Now I want to put in a little warning. You mention that both Dr. Spitz[35] and Dr. Lebovici[36] will be speaking at that conference. As regards Dr. Spitz I have a very bad opinion of him. He wrote his paper on Anaclitic Depression[37] and made an enormous amount of propaganda for himself. He most sharply dissociated his discovery from my work on the Depressive Position and that combination of both stealing from me and attacking me speaks of what I think to be a very bad character. He is everywhere, seems to travel constantly, makes enormous propaganda for himself, and he came to the conclusion that I am not easily discarded, he will be careful about what he says. Dr. Segal knows about him and I am sure will know how to deal with the situation. I do not think anything he appears to have discovered is of any value for reasons I tell you, nor do I believe he has actually an understanding of young children but only uses it for propaganda for himself.

The case of Dr. Lebovici is somewhat different. I know he told me and also others that he found much value in my work, but I have the impression that he has developed on quite different lines. I have no impression that he is malevolent but I really do not know him sufficiently to have an opinion about him. I feel however that he too needs to be dealt with with a certain amount of caution.

All this may not really have to do with you, because if you contribute in the discussion I think // you will probably just speak of your experiences, and that seems to me by far the wisest course to take. What I have told you is only to warn you and not to influence you to try to deal with these two people, which would be much too difficult and which I think is not necessary.

The Centenary celebrations went off very well. I found the ceremony of fixing the plaque very moving and we had a wonderful address from Dr. Jones on the Nature of Greatness[38] on Sunday, and he also spoke on the wireless and appeared on television, and I gather that he gave some very successful lectures in the United States. There are some people who use these occasions for self-advertisement; he is _not_ one of them, but I am glad he got the tributes he so richly deserves.

I was delighted about Dr. de Saussure's invitation to Dr. Segal and also about her being so willing to accept it: the whole thing is the best news I have had for some time and your part in it _is fully appreciated by me and my friends._

I hope your intention to come to London some time will still come true. I am sure it would strengthen your own confidence and probably also be useful _to you_ as

---

35 René A. Spitz (1887-1974) was a psychoanalyst of Hungarian origin. He spent a considerable number of years in Denver, Colorado, USA, where he conducted research into the psychoanalysis of young infants. He taught in Geneva, where he lived in the 1960s.

36 Serge Lebovici (1915-2000) was a French psychoanalyst and professor of child psychiatry.

37 Spitz, R. A. (1946).

38 "The nature of genius" and "Our attitude towards greatness", two of the four addresses to Freud published by Jones, E. (1955). See also Storr, A. (1957).

well as a pleasure to us if you could arrange to come and have conversations with some of us. I can see that the July plan will not now come off, but I hope it will be realised at some other time.

With love

Yours

Melanie Klein

Dr. Heimann[39] is no longer a member of my group. This is well known in England since she made it public that she is now a member of the Independent Group (formerly called // the Middle Group) but this fact is not yet known abroad. This piece of news will come as a surprise and shock to you, – but it was, though very painful, not a great surprise to me. I have seen it coming for years. This is too complex and painful to go into any details about it, but I feel you should know the fact. All my other friends and colleagues stand firmly by me.

---

39 Paula Heimann (1899–1982) was a psychoanalyst who had been analysed by Klein. She became one of Klein's closest colleagues until 1955, when she left the Kleinian Group and joined the Independent (formerly Middle) Group.

Kl 9

20, Bracknell Gardens
London N.W.3

31 July 1956

Chère Madame Spira,

I was delighted with the news Dr. Segal brought home. The success she had was based on the work you have done during the year and I cannot thank you enough for what you are doing. It must also be a great satisfaction to you to have succeeded so well in one year in what seemed to begin with an extremely difficult venture.

Now as regards the papers which I sent you[40] through Dr. Segal. They are actually the ones which you asked for. There are no others in the other volumes of Imago and none of my papers in Imago appeared earlier than 1921. Should you still wish to have them, I can send them at the beginning of September, because I am leaving tomorrow for my holidays and Dr. Segal will also be away. It would be a pity if you were not able to consult the German because, though the English translation is good, I have found it a great advantage also to consider the original. If it does not hold up your work too much, then I would leave it until September.

I am greatly looking forward to my holiday and hope that you, too, will have a good rest: you certainly deserve it after so many exertions.

Should you have any queries to put to me in September I shall be pleased to answer them. In any case we want to discuss the revised translation in the autumn. *Again many thanks and best wishes.*

Yours ever

Melanie Klein

---

40 No further information about these is available at present.

Kl 10, 1-5

20, Bracknell Gardens
London N.W.3

1 October 1956

Chère Mme Spira,

I have to express a very great request for your help. Dr. Boulanger came to see me yesterday on his way from Montreal to Paris where he is going to stay until next summer. He handed me Chapters IX and X of his translation of "The Psycho-Analysis of Children" and told me that he feels that by Christmas he will be able to finish the remaining three chapters. //

If so, he hopes the book will be out in time for the Paris Congress and also it would be an anniversary – 25 years since it appeared in German and English. But, – and this <u>but</u> is of great importance – the footnotes which as you know are very many and some of them dealing with quite important points are not yet translated and he could only finish the book if somebody else would translate them and finish them by Christmas. This, I know, is a very tall order and I am embarrassed to ask you for such // hard work in addition to the one you are already doing. But I know of nobody else who could do this well, - also Dr. Boulanger thinks that Geneva, not being so far from Paris and London would make the possibility for personal discussion more feasible.

I am aware that since you are at work at the Contributions my request would mean interrupting your translation in order to work on the footnotes – all this seems to me // asking a great deal from you. But I am encouraged in doing so by my knowledge that you are deeply and sincerely interested in my work as a whole. There is no doubt that "The Psycho-Analysis of Children" should be the <u>first</u> book to be presented to the French public and it is my impression that if we had to wait for Boulanger to do this it would mean postponing the publication for quite a long time and thus also the publication // of other works in French.

Should you find it possible to translate the footnotes (needless to say that Boulanger mentioned that you would of course be mentioned as one of the translators on the title page). The procedure he suggested is that you should send the translation by and by to him so that the unity in the translation could be preserved. I would see it after he had made, if necessary, his suggestions.

I am keeping well – hard at work and my case history book. I hope you have had good holidays.

Yours ever

Melanie Klein

Kl 11, 1-2

20, Bracknell Gardens
London N.W.3

5 October 1956

Chère Marcelle,

I am writing in a hurry, hoping that this note will still reach you before you leave. I shall arrange for one of my colleagues to bring some material on Monday night. But for our discussions preceding the Monday it would be essential that you should also bring some material (child or/and adult) // because this is very instructive. It need not be a finished paper or something like that but if you would care to report something about your own work you should find this helpful. This was al[l]ways so in my experience. I am particularly thinking about Saturday night when you and I shall have a talk and of Sunday night at Dr. Segal's when we shall be four of us (you, Dr. Segal, Betty Joseph and myself!)

Looking forward to seeing you soon.

Yours

Melanie Klein

Kl 12, 1-2

20, Bracknell Gardens
London N.W.3

12 October 1956

Chère Marcelle,

Your letter gave me great pleasure and lessen[e]d some of my burdens. I am so glad you agree that the first book which should appear in French is "The Psycho-Analysis of Children", and I fully appreciate the great amount of work you are undertaking in translating the footnotes, as well as interrupting the translation of the "Contributions".

Dr. Boulanger was extremely pleased that you are going to co-operate with him and he is getting in touch with Lagache to make possible the publication of the translation by next summer. Dr. Boulanger's address is:

M. le Docteur J. B. Boulanger
11, rue Touillier
Paris (5ème)

I am delighted with the prospect of your coming to London, but would suggest if possible that you should arrive not later than the 14th, since I would wish to give you as much time as possible and I am expecting my sister-in-law on the 17th for a visit prior to her emigrating to Australia later in the month. Should you wish to prolong your stay until the 18th, I could arrange also to give you some time that day.

Apart from the pleasure of seeing you I *would* welcome your visit because it would be of use to you to again get in touch with me and some of my colleagues.

I am very glad to hear that you are so busy and understand fully your difficulties in combining this with reading and writing, but I myself have been very much in that position for many years and I do believe that one cannot neglect either the one or the other. In any case it is a great pleasure to know that your success is growing. //

When you come to London I shall be most interested to hear about the paper on which you are working, and if you could, previous to your visit, send me one or two copies we could possibly also arrange for a few others to discuss it with you.

Believe me that the work you are doing in Switzerland and your support is of great value to me. This, together with the prospect, after 25 years, of having "The Psycho-Analysis of Children", and not too long after that the "Contributions", appear in French is a great compensation, and even happiness, after all the struggle I have gone through for my work.

Yours *with kindest regards,*

Melanie Klein

Kl 13, 1-6

20, Bracknell Gardens
London N.W.3

29 October 1956

Chère Marcelle,

I am delighted with your decision to come to London and the dates suit me very well. In fact it is most convenient that you include a weekend because I have more time then. I shall now suggest for your approval the following arrangements which I discussed with some of my friends: I should be very pleased if you would spend with me Saturday (10th) from the time onwards // when you have arrived at the Cumberland Hotel (It is not at all far from my flat but about this I shall write another time). This would mean that, at about 5–5:30 you would come to me, have dinner with me and that should give us full opportunity for talk and discussion. I should also be glad to see you on Sunday morning for one or two hours. Sunday afternoon and evening Hanna Segal asks you to spend with her. She would, if you like this, // show you something of the country in the afternoon also have you to dinner with her and after dinner Betty Joseph and I would join you at Dr. Segal's house and we could have a discussion Monday night. I should be pleased to have you to dinner. I am free from about 6:30 on and after dinner five or six of my colleagues will come and we can discuss either some material of your own or material which some of us // would provide. Tuesday evening Dr. Segal has a postgraduate Seminar in her house to which you are invited. There will also be some opportunity for you to be present at one or two supervisions on Monday and Tuesday and possibly you could also assist at some work done at the Tavistock Child Therapy courses which work on my lines. Please let me know whether this general outline would suit you or whether you wish some more time free for seeing something of London or of friends in London, also whether you wish to present your paper or some other of your material on Monday night at the meeting in my home or rather have other people presenting their material.

I am writing in bed – it is rather late – but I hope you will be able to read what I wrote in a hurry.

I am greatly looking forward to seeing you so[o]n and so are // my friends.

With Kindest Regards

Yours

Melanie Klein

Kl 14, 1-2

20, Bracknell Gardens
London N.W.3

2 November 1956

Chère Marcelle,

I wish to add a few words to my previous letter, which was written, as I told you, in a hurry.

I take it that you will arrive at the Cumberland Hotel at about 4:30 on Saturday, November 10th, and any time after that I shall be pleased to see you and spend the rest of the afternoon and evening with you, when we might discuss your paper. On Sunday morning, I shall be pleased if you can be here at about 11 o'clock, have lunch with me and after lunch Dr. Segal has, through me, already invited you to spend the afternoon and evening with her. After dinner, Miss Joseph and I will join in your conversation.

I also understand that Dr. Segal has already arranged for you to be present at one child therapy course or some other supervision.

On Monday night I shall be glad to have you to dinner here. I am free from 6:30 onwards and then we shall have a Group Meeting here at which either you can bring material or some of us will bring material.

On Tuesday night Dr. Segal has a seminar which I think will interest you and she shall be pleased if you will go to it.

I am sorry to repeat myself, but having written my earlier letter in bed, late at night, I am not sure whether I made myself clear.

As regards the connection between the Cumberland Hotel and my flat, it is a very simple one. If you come by taxi, you would have to tell the taxi-man that he should not take you up Frognal, but Frognal Lane, which is opposite West End Lane. The first turning on the left from Frognal Lane is Bracknell Gardens, and my // flat, as you know, is in No. 20, flat No. 2 on the first floor. Should you wish to come by bus, a No. 2 bus will take you to West End Lane (Frognal Lane), and they will tell you in the hotel where to get the No. 2 bus.

I can hardly believe that you have, in fact, been able to make the first version of the translation of the footnotes, knowing as I do what an enormous amount of work they involve, and I hope that in the circumstances Boulanger will not find it too difficult to finish the book by the time stated. It will be a very great pleasure to me to actually have "The Psycho-Analysis of Children" appear in French: I had, in the many years during which I have been trying to get the right translators, nearly given up hope that it ever would.

I shall be most interested in the paper which you want to discuss with me and, as I said, which you might also wish to discuss with the Group on Monday, when some of my closest colleagues will be present too, but about that I expect your reply.

Yours *with best wishes*

Melanie Klein

P.S. Since I wrote to you and dictated this letter I have heard that my family [is] [are] *going next Sunday to Cambridge to visit my grandson*[41] *and since I am longing to see the boy I would like to take this opportunity and go with them. Miss Betty Joseph would be delighted if instead of coming to me on Sunday you went to see her at 11:30 and stay for lunch there. You will find a talk with her interesting and useful. I hope you will forgive me for that change* [change] *of plans.*

41 Michael Clyne, Eric's son.

Kl 15

Flat 2, 20, Bracknell Gardens
London N.W.3

7 December 1956

Chère Marcelle,

This is only to thank you for your letter. It is not [through] politeness that I reply that we were all delighted to have you here and were sorry you could not stay longer, nor is it façon de parler[42] if I say that I am most grateful for the work you are doing and now in particular that you are going to take care of the translation of the "Psycho-Analysis of Children".

I have not heard from Boulanger and I think there cannot be a hope that this man is going to finish the translation. It would be wrong for me to be too much influenced by personal reasons and I think I shall have to tell him that I cannot wait any longer. I do not think I should leave you with that difficult situation, though possibly your suggestion that you have to translate the chapters any way for your own use would be helpful, but I feel since we are now near the New Year when the book was to have been finished, I shall write to him that I would wish you to finish it.

I am so glad you feel this should be finished before the Contributions and that you are willing to interrupt this work in order to help me in the matter.

I am glad that you feel your stay in London was refreshing for you and hope we shall soon see you for a longer time here.

With all good wishes for Christmas,

Yours *ever*

Melanie Klein

---

42 In French in the original.

Kl 16, 1-2

20, Bracknell Gardens
London N.W.3

4 February 1957

Chère Marcelle,

It is quite some time since I have heard from you. I hope you had a pleasant and restful Christmas holiday, but assume you have been back at work for some time. I am working very hard indeed on the book which you know about, the Case History of a Child. At the same time I am expecting any minute to receive the proofs of my book Envy and Gratitude, and though I have a friend who will read it I have also to read it myself. In addition to that I am now going through the translations of Boulanger's 9th and 10th chapters and what he has sent me since the New Year – the Prefaces, half of the 12th chapter and the 13th chapter. I am now much more content since only the 11th chapter – a very difficult one – and half of the 12th chapter and the Index are missing. I can now see the translation actually coming to an end.

Boulanger had put some questions to me: I send you my answers to them because you might find them useful in your translation of the footnotes. I should be very glad to know how far you have revised these footnotes. I understood that you were going to revise them and then send them on to Boulanger, and now when he is actually coming nearer to the end of the translation it would be a blessing if he also had your revised footnotes.

You were quite right – the number of the Imago[43] which I sent you was not the right one and I shall see if I cannot find that first paper in German as you ask me. Should I find it I shall send it on to you, but that is something which I know now takes second place after the footnotes.

I seem full of requests today, because I am now going to ask you something else. I am rather keen to arrange my summer holidays and having made enquiries have come to the conclusion that a holiday in France is expensive and not good. I am very keen to be in a French part of Switzerland and should like to find a quiet place // in a good second-class hotel, quietly situated, with a *nice* garden and a deck-chair in which I can rest. Do you think you can make enquiries about this? I know it seems still early but my experience two years ago has shown me that it is necessary to book quite a number of months ahead and I should be glad to have my summer holidays settled.

I hope that everything is all right with you and that your silence is only due to being very busy. I should however be very glad to hear from you soon.

Yours *ever*

Melanie Klein

---

43 No further information about these is available at present.

Kl 17

20, Bracknell Gardens
London N.W.3

14 February 1957

Chère Marcelle,

I am a bit worried to have had no news from you for what is relatively quite a long time.

I wrote to you ten days ago, but am not absolutely sure whether my letter was correctly addressed, so I am enclosing a copy in case the original letter has gone astray.

I should be glad to have a few lines from you to let me know how you are: I hope you are not ill or having any other trouble.

Yours *ever*

Melanie Klein

Kl 18, 1-2 (copy of the letter of 4 February with additional comments)

Chère Marcelle,

It is quite some time since I have heard from you. I hope you had a pleasant and restful Christmas holiday, but assume you have been back at work for some time. I am working very hard indeed on the book which you know about, the Case History of a Child[44]. At the same time I am expecting any minute to receive the proofs of my book Envy and Gratitude, and though I have friends who will read it I have also to read it myself. In addition to that I am now going through the translations of Boulanger's 9th and 10th chapters and what he has sent me since the New Year – the Prefaces, half of the 12th chapter and the 13th chapter. I am now much more content since only the 11th chapter – a very difficult one – and half of the 12th chapter and the Index are missing. I can now see the translation actually coming to an end.

Boulanger had put some questions to me: I send you my answers to them because you might find them useful in your translation of the footnotes. I should be very glad to know how far you have revised these footnotes. I understood that you were going to revise them and then send them on to Boulanger, and now when he is actually coming nearer to the end of the translation it would be a blessing if he also had your revised footnotes.

You were quite right – the number of the Imago which I sent you was not the right one and I shall see if I cannot find that first paper in German as you ask me. Should I find it I shall send it on to you, but that is something which I [k]now takes second place after the footnotes.

I seem full of requests today, because I am now going to ask you something else. I am rather keen to arrange my summer holidays and having made enquiries have come to the conclusion that a holiday in France is expensive and not good. I am very keen to be in a French part of Switzerland and should like to find a quiet place in a good second-class hotel, quietly situated, with a garden and a deck-chair in which I can rest. Do you think you can make enquiries about this? I know it seems still early but my experience two years ago has shown me that it is necessary to book quite a number of months ahead and I should be glad to have my summer holidays settled.

I hope that everything is all right with you and that your silence is only due to being very busy. I should however be very glad to hear from you soon.

Yours //

1.   I agree to "figure composite des parents" as preferable to the other suggestions and the reasons which you give me for this choice are quite valid.

---

44 Klein, M. (1961).

2. I also agree to "sadique-anal".

3. As regards the question of demarcation between the different stages of development, it seems necessary according to the context to speak of "bébés", or "up to 2 years", "up to 3 years", or as the context shows. I do find differentiation between the very young child and the somewhat older one quite important. Occasionally I think one could also use "petits enfants" or "enfants à bas age", but I agree with you that it would not be good to use it regularly.

4. I agree to "morcellement" in preference to "fragmentation".

5. The question of describing the oral stage is more complicated. I agree to the use of "le stade oral de succion" and "le stade oral de morsure" wherever I refer to the oral sucking and the oral biting stage, but wish the expression "sadique-oral" and "sadique-urethral" to be used wherever I refer to these in the original.

Kl 19, 1-2

20, Bracknell Gardens
London N.W.3

22 February 1957

Chère Marcelle,

The day after I wrote to you I received your letter, for which many thanks. I was sorry to hear that your situation is not easy, but actually I never expected it to be and since, as I hope, your time is still occupied, I think you can leave further solutions to time. It would of course be very nice if you received your Membership, but if you do not get it I do not think it will prevent people from appreciating your work. I am telling you this from experience, though of course when I came to England I had Dr. Jones' very strong support, but nevertheless, I have come fully to the conviction that good work wins in the end. I am now getting from all sorts of places in the United States signs of interest and expressions of the wish to learn, and this is from people who have no direct contact with me as the Swiss *now* have with you.

I am afraid I cannot any more be sure about the paper you sent me two years ago. I take it that at the time I made some suggestions to you and you will probably remember whether I suggested you send it to the International Journal of Psycho-Analysis. If I did, I repeat that suggestion. The second paper you mention, which goes back some years, would be very interesting but I would suggest to you to revise it perhaps in the light of what you have since seen in your work. If you care then to send it to me I shall give you an opinion, or possibly discuss it with one or two friends of mine.

I have just received your second letter containing the various prospectuses: thank you very much. I have not yet been able to study then, but what I am very keen on is to go to a place 1,000 to 1,200 or 1,300 meters up, but not more, and to be recommended a good hotel, because in the prospectuses they all look as beautiful as can be and one cannot be sure that one has a nice room with a balcony and a pleasant view, and a garden – things which are very essential for me.

I do not know of course whether you can find such a hotel because I realise you have to rely on the agency where you // get the prospectuses, but if by any chance you could find such *a personal* recommendation, I should be very grateful.

The book on Envy and Gratitude[45] is coming out in a few weeks' time and that no doubt will give me courage to finish the book in hand. I have announced a Congress paper with a splendid title "On the Development of Mental Functioning"[46], and am quite afraid of what I am undertaking. After Easter I must stop everything in order to produce a paper which is worthy of that title *or at least not quite unworthy of it.*

With my very best wishes and thanks,

Yours, *ever*

Melanie Klein

---

45 Klein, M. (1957).
46 Klein, M. (1958).

Kl 20, 1-2

20, Bracknell Gardens
London N.W.3

7 March 1957

Chère Marcelle,

Many thanks for your letter and for the trouble you have taken in finding accommodation for me. Will you be so kind as to book the room in the Hotel Beau Rivage at Château D'Oex. I shall arrive on the 2nd August and would like to stay until 26th August. I assume there will be no difficultly in my not staying a month, which would be inconvenient for me, and also too expensive, since the Swiss franc is now only 12 to the pound. I take it that I understood you right that the room faces south and has a balcony. I hope the hotel is not too small, because there is more opportunity of finding some company in a larger one. I assume also that there is running hot and cold water in the room and it does not matter that there is no private bathroom. Another point which I hope will be all right is that the room is not too high up. Of course, if there is a lift this does not matter, but if there is not it would be difficult for me to go higher than the first floor: in fact, I like being on the first floor.

I hear that Château d'Oex is charming and the height is just right for me and since you mention that the hotel is comfortable, that is all I really want.

You do not mention anything about your two papers[47]. I hope that is only because you were on holiday, because you must not think I am not sufficiently interested in them. My memory is not good and I would not even be quite sure what I said about my own paper two years ago, so if you wish me to give an opinion and can remind me about what I said two years ago, I wish still to keep to what I said in my letter.

With many thanks,

Yours ever, Melanie Klein

P.S. I have just rung the Swiss Tourist Office to find out about the connection between Paris and Château d'Oex. //

P.T.O. and they say there is no Hôtel Beau Rivage in Château d'Oex: can I have misread the name in your letter? I shall be very glad to have this summer holiday fixed.

It is likely that this hotel is not on the guide list for reasons of their own.

---

47 No further information about these is available at present.

Kl 21, 1-2

Flat 2, 20, Bracknell Gardens
London N.W.3

21 March 1957

Chère Marcelle,

Thank you very much for your letter. I am very pleased with the hotel you have chosen for me: it all looks very pleasant and I am greatly looking forward to a holiday which I am sure I shall need after the Congress. Before the Congress I shall get very tired because I am working extremely hard on my paper which I am finding difficult and I shall have to write and re-write it several times.

Thank you for your kind invitation to stay with you for a few days after my holiday. I accept this invitation with pleasure. This might also be a good occasion to discuss your papers.

And now I am coming with another S.O.S. As we both knew, the translation of "The Psycho-Analysis of Children" would not be ready by the time Boulanger thought, but in any case I have the second half of the 12th chapter, which leaves only the 11th chapter – a very heavy one – and the Index still to be translated. Boulanger had intended to hand over the translation of the book to Lagache at the end of February, but I am not disappointed because I never believed this would be possible. Boulanger has appealed to me to ask you whether you would undertake the translation of the Index and he would then go through it himself. I asked him to write to you directly about it, since you had offered to help him at the time you met in Paris, but I am not sure whether he actually wrote to you. In a note I have had from him he seems a bit disturbed: he also refers to personal matters which delayed the translation and I am very sorry for him.

Now, could you make this new sacrifice and translate the Index? My own feeling is that if he gets this assurance he will in fact finish the translation // of the 11th chapter and then at last the book will be finished. It is the one I decided to revise myself and I have done so, although at times I found it very difficult to fit in, but since it is my fundamental book and, years ago, I promised the Boulangers I would revise it, I felt I must keep my promise. It is an enormous relief to have the translation finished, which in fact has taken longer than the actual writing of the book, but it is extremely difficult to translate and Boulanger has done it very well. I am quite sure that later on it will be immaterial to me that it took a year longer, because it is the quality of the translation which counts.

Should you really be able to tackle the Index would you kindly get in touch with Boulanger directly and tell him so? He is leaving Paris on the 31st March and spends the day with me, and I believe it would be very helpful if, before he comes to see me, he already knew whether or not you could give him help with the Index. *Please forgive me to ask you again to do work, when you are already so busy.*

With all good wishes,

Yours *ever*

Melanie Klein

P.S. Do you want me to confirm directly to the hotel that I would like them to book my room from the 2nd to 26th August, so that I could also have their *written* assurance that this has been done?

Kl 22, 1-2

Flat 2, 20, Bracknell Gardens
London N.W.3

5 April 1957

Chère Marcelle,

I was very glad to receive your letter with the good news that you are now a psycho-analyst acknowledged by the Swiss Association[48], and I have no doubt your next paper will have the end result that you are aiming at. I am very interested in the topic of your paper, but I am afraid I am not particularly good at literature, which I have neglected for some time in order to write my own papers.

I thank you also very much for the reservation at the hotel, and I shall repay the deposit you made when I see you. In order to book my return ticket from Geneva I had to decide about the time I shall spend with you. I have booked the ticket for the 29th August: I hope that this is in keeping with your plans.

Boulanger came to see me last Sunday and he was going to write to you to thank you for the Notes. He left a copy of them with me, but I see no possibility at the moment of revising them because I am deeply immersed in my Congress paper and the contribution which I have promised to make to the discussion on the Direct Observation of the Child[49]. It is very kind of you that you *agreed* to contribute to the Index and it is essential that Boulanger discusses with you the details. I have written to him about that but perhaps, since he tends to postpone matters, it might be as well if you wrote to him to his address in Montreal: he has gone back there for a month. His address is:

Dr. J.B. Boulanger
4050 chemin de la Côte St. Catherine
Montréal 26, Canada

He promised me the 11th chapter, which is still missing, within a few weeks and that and the Index are the only // things missing so that I am hopeful the translation will at last be finished. I am quite sure that without your translating the Notes it might still have been prolonged indefinitely: it was a very big task to accomplish and I thank you very much for that.

I am just on the point of leaving for a fortnight's holiday which I shall spend in Holland and it is particularly pleasant for me that my grandson comes with me[50]. With good luck the weather will hold and then it should be a very pleasant holiday.

Again many thanks for your contributions,

Yours *ever*

Melanie Klein

---

48 Swiss Psychoanalytical Society.
49 Unpublished.
50 Michael Clyne, Eric's son.

Kl 23, 1-2

Flat 2, 20, Bracknell Gardens
London N.W.3

9 May 1957

Chère Marcelle,

I should be glad to know whether my suggestion to stay with you from the 26th to 29th August is convenient. I know that at the beginning of September you go to the Child Psychiatric Congress and that is why I decided to go home on the 29th, but I am not sure whether you might not have some preparations to make and whether I am holding you up by staying until the 29th.

I have heard from Boulanger that he is sending me the first half of the 11th chapter, which means that only the second half of this chapter and the Index have to be done. Now the Index is a cause of great concern: it cannot be simply translated from the English or German. I know that you are very overburdened and you have already done, and are doing, a great deal for me. It might be necessary to get a professional index maker for this. These people, though skilled, do not know the work and that was always the reason why I tried to get somebody who knew the work to help with it. What is your opinion about this? *Perhaps one could translate the Index from the English?* Since the announcement that at last I am to get the first half of the 11th chapter, this indicates that some time or other I shall also get the other half and I should like to prepare in my mind what should be done about the Index and Boulanger, though he mentioned it to me, did not make any particular suggestions, except that he hoped for your help. Whether he has conveyed that hope to you or not, I do not know.

I am getting on with my Congress paper and have still to work out a contribution to the discussion on Observation of the Child. I am so far not entirely satisfied with the way I express my views on such a fundamental matter as the Development of Mental Functioning, but I shall have to be satisfied if I can convey my thoughts, which I think I am doing. //

I had a very pleasant Easter holiday in Holland with my grandson, but though very interesting and enjoyable it was not particularly restful. It was a great pleasure to me to be with him and also to see again beautiful paintings, a world from which I have more or less excluded myself of recent years because it is so tiring. I shall take some days off at Whitsun and that I hope will be more restful.

Are you preparing your paper for membership?

The book on Envy and Gratitude will be out on the 7th June and I shall send you a copy when it appears. The layout is beautiful and I am very pleased with it.

Yours *ever*

Melanie Klein

Kl 24

Flat 2, 20, Bracknell Gardens
London N.W.3

16 May 1957

Chère Marcelle,

I was delighted when I saw from your letter that you have actually already made the Index. I have no doubt that there is room for improvement in the Index of the English edition and I should be very interested indeed to see the index you have made. If you could send me a copy, I hope within a week or two to be able to go through it.

I am just about to revise the first half of the 11th chapter which Boulanger sent me, so if we can actually finish the Index, then there is very little left, because he promises me to send the second half of the chapter very soon. Of course, he too will have to see the index, but I feel that this time I would like to have a look at it as well.

It is a wonderful thought that this book is really going to be finished against all odds.

I am very glad that the dates of my arrival in Geneva and departure suit you and I am looking forward to the time I shall spend with you.

Yours ever

Melanie Klein

Kl 25

Flat 2, 20, Bracknell Gardens
London N.W.3

21 June 1957

Chère Marcelle,

You have given me great pleasure indeed by your letter, because it showed a deep understanding of something in my work and attitude which I think very few people would particularly connect with this book. I am also very glad to see that you use it already in your work and you should not be discouraged if that particular patient – and I think I can guess who it is – does not give the result hoped for, but we can discuss that in detail when we are together in Geneva.

I thought it might be useful for you and for the work if I addressed a number of colleagues during my stay in Geneva. The best date would be August 27th because the 28th is the last day before I leave, but I could manage [*on that day*] if you found that day more suitable. I do not, of course, know whether anybody will be in Geneva at this time, but should they be and should you favour this idea, I would be quite willing to speak to them, as long as it is understood that I am not preparing a paper for that occasion. I am very burdened with my preparations for the Congress, and my paper does not seem to be progressing as well as I should like; I have also to speak in a discussion on Child Observation. Nevertheless, [*in spite*] of all this and a number of extra commitments which I still have during this month (it is the season when the Americans come to London), I am keeping well.

Looking forward to meeting you in Paris,

Yours

Melanie Klein

Kl 26, 1-2

Flat 2, 20, Bracknell Gardens
London N.W.3

20 July 1957

Chère Marcelle,

I am writing in a great hurry. I should be glad if you could bring with you to Paris the MS of "Envy and Gratitude" which I gave you when you were in London. For certain reasons I should be very glad if you had kept it and could let me have it *back.*

You may have heard from Boulanger that now the book is to go to the publisher on the 10th August and he hopes to discuss with you some points about the Index during the Congress.

Let me thank you again for the very timely help you gave both with the footnotes and the Index, the book would otherwise have taken still longer before going to the publishers.

I have at last finished my Congress paper, but am very tired indeed and am not in a position to say whether it is good or not. I am now making a few notes about Child Observation.

I hope still to get a few days' rest before the Congress, which will no doubt make great demands on me. //

If you have not yet made any other plans, Boulanger would like to have me and a few friends to an informal afternoon tea on the Wednesday, and I should be glad if you could be with us.

Looking forward to seeing you,

Yours *ever*

Melanie Klein

Kl 27, 1-2

Hôtel Beau-Séjour
Château-d'Oex
W. Muller-Casutt
Tél. (029) 46423

17 August 1957

Dear Marcelle,

I hope you have had a very interesting and satisfactory holiday and are going to return home well rested.

I have had a good holiday here and am well rested. Unfortunately, we have had the last week continuously rain and it was very lucky that I have had very pleasant company. To-day the sun is shining again.

I am now writing to // ask you whether you would care to come here for three days and stay with me here as my guest. If, say, you arrived here on the 23rd August we could return together to Geneva on the 26th as was arranged. If this suggestion is to your liking and fits in with you[r] arrangements I would suggest that you bring with you the Index and the footnotes of "The Psycho-Analysis of Children" as well as the English book and we could spend a few hours [every day] to go through it. It was quite impossible for me to do so beforehand but now, together, it would be easy. I know you would like me to look into it. It is very much on my mind that there should be nothing to prevent the translation to go to the publishers and – another matter – I should very much enjoy to spend here a few days in your company.

With Kindest Regards

Yours

Melanie Klein

Kl 28, 1-2

20, Bracknell Gardens
London N.W.3

30 August 1957

I am posting the Ind[e]x to you tomorrow

Dear Marcelle,

I had a very good journey and to-day I am spending quietly in bed; by to-morrow I shall be completely rested.

My thanks to you for the lovely hospitality you gave me are very warmly experienced. I enjoyed these days in Geneva and in your beautiful home very much indeed and I am going over the details in my mind with great pleasure and with gratitude both for your loyalty towards my work and what is more, your real understanding of it and also – what I feel your warm personal feelings towards me which I value and reciprocate.

It is a great relief to me to think that the Index is now finished and I do hope that Boulanger will take trouble over the footnotes and not prolong this much longer. I was also pleased to see him again – I am very grateful for the work he has done and I also like him personally – the time we three spent together was very pleasant, too. Please tell your friend that I was very pleased to meet her and greatly enjoyed seeing this beautiful house.

With love yours

Melanie Klein

Give my regards and thanks please to Geneva who has been very nice towards me.

Kl 29

Flat 2, 20, Bracknell Gardens
London N.W.3

6 September 1957

Chère Marcelle,

I am enclosing two reviews of "Envy and Gratitude"[51] which I thought might interest you. You need not return them.

I have settled down to work again, feeling it a bit much at the beginning, but that is usual – I need a week or two to get myself completely settled.

I have already started on my next project – the story of the analysis of the small boy. It is going to make a very voluminous book.

I am still thinking about the fact that our thoughts on Unconscious Memory should have met in the way they did. The only explanation, as you suggested, is that we must fundamentally very much think on similar lines.

I am writing to Lagache about the publication and shall let you know his answer.

I keep a very pleasant memory about my stay with you and Geneva has now very much gained in my estimation. I really think it is a lovely town. I must tell you that the presents I brought home were an enormous success: everyone was pleased and I have no doubt that your help in selecting them contributed to that success.

Yours ever

Melanie Klein

---

51 *Why are they Angry? Envy and Gratitude*, by Melanie Klein (Tavistock Publications). Book review John Howard. *The Spectator*, August 10th, 1957. *Envy and Gratitude: A Study of Unconscious*, by Melanie Klein (Tavistock Publications). (Book review not signed). *The Listener*, June 27th, 1957.

Kl 30, 1-2

Flat 2, Bracknell Gardens
20, London N.W.3

25 October 1957

Chère Marcelle,

Thank you for your letter and I can reassure you that my not having written to you earlier was not due to my health being in any way impaired. It is due to the fact that in addition to my work there are always a lot of problems cropping up and, as you know, I have to have enough rest to keep going, and so at such times my correspondence suffers.

I know from Boulanger that he thinks very well of the Index, therefore he must have received it but you know that he is rather dilatory about acknowledging things.

I had a letter from Lagache who wishes, as usually, to help me, but he feels that even his influence may not help to get the other two books—the Contributions and the Developments—published as quickly as we might wish. On the other hand he says, quite rightly, that they are not yet finished, though you assure me that your translation will not take much time to be completed. I remember though that you said you would carefully go over the whole translation again and Lagache indicates that careful revision of a translation is a necessity, so if you feel like taking up the translation again it may be helpful because it would give you an opportunity to revise it a second time and then I could give a date when it will be ready.

Lagache says he would be very sorry if we chose another publisher, but he will only be guided by my wish. Now, I do not feel that at my age I should agree to the translations appearing in 2 or 3 years' time. On the other hand, Lagache says that if he mentions that I might get another publisher, the leading editor at the Presses Universitaires[52] may agree to publishing the books earlier because he may not like another firm to take over. Lagache says he thinks it will be quite easy for me to find another publisher, and that is really what I am inclined to do. Since you have heard good opinions of Payot I would wish to get in touch with him, or would you do that in my name since it needs faultless French, which I am not sure that I can provide. You can say that this translation is authorised by me and that the publication rights are with the Hogarth Press[53]. We must not neglect that because it is very important to get permission for the translation and the publication from the Hogarth Press, but that is probably something quite usual for the publisher and will not be any difficulty. So I think, chère Marcelle, if you would get in touch with Payot we could get an idea whether and when he would be willing to publish the books and that also implies that you could fix a date when you will finish.

I remember with pleasure my holiday and my very pleasant stay in your home, but it seems all so far away now.

Yours *ever*

Melanie Klein

---

52 Presses Universitaires de France, Paris.
53 The publishers in Great Britain of the Standard Edition of the Complete Psychological Works of Sigmund Freud.

Kl 31

20, Bracknell Gardens
London N.W.3

19 December 1957

Chère Marcelle,

I was glad to have your letter and to know that you are well and that matters seem to be satisfactory. You do not give me any details about the prospect of your becoming a member of the Swiss Society, but I gather that this will come in time, in spite of everything.

I wish to congratulate you heartily on the marriage of your son[54] and I am glad to know that you feel that he will be happy. Since you are looking forward to grandchildren, I hope this will come true in due time. I myself derive the greatest pleasure from my grandchildren – satisfaction about work is of quite a different nature, and has a good deal to do also with feelings of duty, that I have to do my best to keep this work alive. My conviction is strong enough to make all sorts of difficulties put in my way bearable or even sometimes insignificant.

I am very glad to hear that you expect to finish the translation by the summer. I know that this is hard work and therefore needs time. I have written to Lagache and asked his advice about another publisher. The trouble is, of course, that my name is not sufficiently known in France, but I feel that will come after we get some of the translations published. My books are now selling quite well in the United States in spite of the difficulties which have been put in my way there.

I am keeping quite well, but am tired and am therefore looking forward to a fortnight's holiday.

I wish you a very happy Christmas and New Year and please give my congratulations also to your son.

Yours ever

Melanie Klein

---

54 Gilbert Schwob.

Kl 32, 1-2

2/20, Bracknell Gardens
London N.W.3

10 January 1958

Madame Marcelle Spira
5, Rond Point de Plainpalais
Geneva, SWITZERLAND

Chère Marcelle,

I hope that you had a pleasant holiday. I was very satisfied with mine and feel more rested.

Thank you for having written to Payot. I have asked Lagache whom else he could recommend and I enclose his reply. Please return it to me. As you see, he is not against our trying somebody else. Would you kindly get in touch with one of the publishers he mentions, and it might be useful when you write to mention that my book "The Psycho-Analysis of Children" has appeared in its sixth edition in English and is selling very well in the Spanish translation.

I was very pleased to hear that your son is happy and is going to be married. Will you please give him and his bride my very best wishes for their happiness.

You have not told me about your membership paper[55]. Have you any plans when you are going to read it? It is good news that, in spite of the difficulties which are no doubt increased through the French child analysts, you are not losing courage. I have come to the conclusion that all these personal matters and difficulties, of which we have also plenty in this Society here, are not important and can be counteracted by good books appearing. My book is getting on and [*I hear "Env*]y and Gratitude" is selling very well, and there are two or [*three oth*]er books in preparation, by Dr. Segal, Dr. Bion[56] and also, I [*hear, by*] Dr. Rosenfeld. Your personal influence, your knowledge and [*your deter*]mination should also carry great weight. I am glad to see [*that you*] share my feeling that nothing, in the long run, is going to [*prevent th*]e truth. After many years of difficulties, I have not lost [*confidence*] and I am happy to find that my younger colleagues develop [*the same*] attitude. I am after all not sending you [*Lagache's*] letter but shall give you the names of editors he suggested:

55 Spira, M. (1959). Accepted in 1958, the paper was published in the *Revue Française de Psychanalyse* in 1959.
56 Wilfred R. Bion (1897–1979).

L'Arche,
27, rue Saint André des Arts
Paris (VI)

Desclée de Brower et Cie
65 bis, rue des Saints-Pères
Paris (VII)

[*Lagache*] writes that when the translation by you [*is*] [be] finished, he will be in a better position [*to start*] [at] the discussion with the Presses Universitaires. //

He also writes (I hope not only to comfort me) that my name is well known in France not necessarily by publishers but at least by the interested public. It is a pity that Boulanger is not any more in Paris to connect and get in touch with publishers personally which Baranger thinks would be a great advantage. Lagache believes that the commercial prospects are good and it is necessary to point this out to the publisher.

With all good wishes for 1958

Yours ever

Melanie Klein

Kl 33, 1-3

20, Bracknell Gardens
London N.W.3

31 January 1958

Chère Marcelle,

Thank you for your letter. I am glad to hear that you feel happy about the marriage of your son, and there is no need to say that I understand all your feelings in that connection.

I realise that the most important thing for you to do now is to finish your paper for membership. I shall be most interested to hear from you as to how it went off and what effect it had. I am glad that you take so much trouble over it, and re-read and reformulate, because I know from my own experience that that will very likely improve the paper. It is most annoying that Diatkine[57] and Lebovici are so disturbing and unfortunately have an influence on the Swiss, who actually know so little that they are liable not to be able to discriminate.

It would be a great advantage if your paper could appear in the Revue de Psychoanalyse Française. I am sorry that the publication of my paper on Symbol Formation in the Lagache review may have been in the way of your paper being published in the Revue Française. I had grave doubts at the time and refused to do so when Lagache asked me to make any footnotes or corrections, because I thought that, since the paper had been written so many years ago, it would not matter much, but I see that I should simply have refused to have it published there. Since then I had a very frank exchange of views with Lagache, telling him that I did not wish to be involved in any way with his group and that my relation with him was based purely on a personal friendship; I had a very understanding answer from him, in which he said that he understood that I wanted to look after my own garden. Quite recently, Baranger told me that the Lagache review wanted to publish one of the chapters of my "Contributions", and I definitely declined that publication. It is possible that if de Saussure actually enquires about having your paper published in the Revue Française, they might accept it. They are not well disposed towards me and my work, otherwise more than, I think, two papers of mine would have appeared in that Revue. // On the other hand, it is possible that they do not want to show this openly. I had a good deal of correspondence about the publication of some of my papers with Madame Bonaparte's secretary, and the excuse they gave was that they had no time to translate.

Should the Revue Française not accept the paper, then it would have to be published by the International Journal of Psycho-Analysis, but needs a really good

---

57   René Diatkine (1918-1997) was a French psychoanalyst who, *inter alia*, developed child analysis in Paris as well as in Geneva, where he taught regularly.

translation. If it comes to that, I shall talk myself to Hoffer[58], who, since the incident at the Congress, is doubly keen not to affront me in any way, and I do not believe he will refuse the publication of your paper. Of course, the translation into English is not as useful to you in Switzerland as a French publication, in the official review, but, on the other hand, it would introduce you to the English and American public, so that I am not sure that it would be such a disadvantage. One can even think of the possibility that, if your paper is accepted by the Revue, it could concurrently appear in the Journal.

Your feeling about an approach to other publishers is quite justified. Baranger also expressed doubts about a written approach and suggested that I should have a more important recommendation, or, if possible, a personal contact with one of the publishers. Although Lagache says that my name is known in France, my impression is that it is not particularly known to publishers. So we have to go carefully about such an approach, so, as not to get another refusal. Unfortunately, I cannot ask Lagache to support me in this matter, because that would not be in keeping with his relation to the Presses Universitaires. I do not know that a letter from the Hogarth Press would have much influence, so I am at the moment quite uncertain w[h]ich way to choose. If I could approach them personally, it would be different, but that is really not possible for me. I am no longer enterprising enough to make a journey to Paris for that reason. I may ask Lagache's advice, though, as I say, he cannot directly intervene for the publication. Perhaps one of us will have an idea what to do. I shall also write to Baranger about this, who, I know, gives serious thought to this question. //

I am glad to think that, after you have finished your paper, you will take up the translation again. As I have already told you, Lagache thinks that in the autumn he might be able to press the translation with the Presses Universitaires. As you will remember, he thought that, if I could refer to the possibility of another publication, it would carry more weight.

I am keeping well and am looking forward to my Easter holidays with my grandchildren.

With best wishes

Yours ever

Melanie Klein

---

58 Willi Hoffer (1897–1967) was editor of *The International Journal of Psycho-Analysis*, 1949–1959.

Kl 34

20, Bracknell Gardens
London N.W.3

17 March 1958

Chère Marcelle,

I assume that you are very busy with your paper and I know from experience that then one is not very inclined towards correspondence. I think, however, that I should let you know that I have heard from Lagache that there is no prospect of the Presses Universitaires publishing any further translations. I shall have, therefore, to get in touch with the two firms whose addresses I sent you.

I shall also write to Baranger. He might have someone in Paris who could make personal introductions to these people. After all, he comes from Paris and he is very keen to have both your translation and his own published.

I have an idea that at this time you are about to read your paper and, should this be so, I am sending you my very best wishes. I hope to hear from you after that is over.

I am keeping well on the whole, but the winter does not quite agree with me and I had two or three weeks during which I was not so well, – not serious though.

With best wishes

Yours ever

Melanie Klein

Kl 35, 1-4

20, Bracknell Gardens
London N.W.3

13 June 1958

Chère Marcelle,

I was very glad to have your letter, all the more so as one of mine to you had not been answered. I quite realize that you are very busy and how easy it is then to put aside one's correspondence. I was extremely pleased to hear from you again.

I have been for months without any answer from Boulanger and the book has gone completely to sleep. In my despair, I asked Lagache, who is really very helpful, to enquire about it, and he was told that a contract between Presses Universitaires and Boulanger had never been answered by Boulanger. Lagache suggested to them that they should start with the printing in spite of this. After another S.O.S. to Boulanger, I at last got an answer, which explained perhaps why he had not received the contract; he has changed his address. He writes that he has sent a telegram to the Presses Universitaires, asking them to send him the contract again, but to start printing at once. I sometimes wonder whether this book is ever going to come out. I believe I shall need a very long life to see it printed.

I had asked Lagache for advice about publishers for the other books and he got in touch with Desclée de Brouwer et Cie, mentioning, as it happens, the publication of the Developments. As they wrote to me to say that, after the warm recommendation of Dr. Lagache, they are inclined to publish this book, I stuck to the suggestion made by Lagache, that is to say, to the publication of the Developments first, which, in the meantime, Baranger has nearly finished. This does not mean that we [s]hall not find somebody, perhaps even the same firm, for the Contributions, and therefore, chère Marcelle, I suggest that you do not give up the translation, but finish it as soon as your time allows. I know that you intend to go through the whole translation again and I know too how much time that takes. Lagache even thought it possible // that the Presses Universitaires might accept another translation which may be a way of getting the Contributions in, but in any case, we are not giving up the search, and Baranger is going to establish a personal connection with Payot, which he thought preferable to any letters we could write. All this means that you are not to be discouraged from finishing the Contributions, because I have it very much at heart that this book should be published and I shall not rest until it is.

I am very interested in your plans to expand your ideas about time and space, and I am looking forward to reading the paper you sent me. Since my Whitsun[59] holiday, I have been extremely busy, among other things, entertaining my

---

59 Whitsun (or Whit Sunday) is the usual term in English for Pentecost.

American publisher and his wife, and some other Americans, etc., but I hope that by now things will be a little quieter, and I shall be able to enjoy your paper.

Since I cannot live without writing, I have made a feeble attempt towards starting a Congress paper, but, as usual, the beginning is difficult for me, in spite of my having quite a lot of thoughts on the topic. However, this is such a usual procedure for me that it does not discourage me. I wish I could do as Freud did, that is, sit down and write a paper which I had already beforehand fully worked out in my head, but it is never like that for me, because a good deal of work enters while I am beginning to write. I have also other topics in mind, but these must be left for a little.

I had a wonderful holiday [i]n South Wales, with very good weather and [a] pleasant hospitality from friends, which made it very enjoyable. It has given me quite a lift, so I hope to be able to keep on without getting too tired until the summer holidays. There are plenty of problems at this time of the year, because we are nearing the election, and there always seem other demands made on me, from which I cannot withdraw, partly because it is impossible and partly because I do not want to, but there is no doubt that they tire me more than actual work.

I am sorry to hear that your position among your Swiss colleagues is still so difficult and I am fully in sympathy with the isolation in which you are as far as work is concerned, but I am not in the least surprised. //

Your undertaking to introduce real analysis into Switzerland is such difficult and important pioneer work that it would be surprising if it were easier than it has turned out to be. I wish you had one or two colleagues who would join you in Switzerland. Miss Everson[60], who visited me, made a very good impression; it is a pity that she does not seem to intend to leave [the] Argentin[a]. It is very difficult to stand by oneself, and it needs a great deal of courage and strength, but I believe you have these two qualities and therefore I do not doubt that in the end you will come through. The great thing is that you have patience. I myself have experienced so much isolation that I can fully sympathise with your position. Even now, when I have a number of capable and reliable colleagues to share my work, the feeling of isolation has by no means gone. In a society where I have worked for 32 years, I can still find a striking lack of understanding and good-will in the majority of colleagues. My answer to their lack of interest, to their envy and jealousy, was always to write and, as it happens, in spite of the controversial position in which I still am, there is no doubt that my work is making its way. Again and again, I get confirmation of this. Jones used to tell me "Truth must come through" but truth has the quality of being inconvenient and therefore one has to be resigned to the fact that it is always only a minority that can accept it. However, this minority is of great importance.

---

60 No further information is available concerning this person.

I am telling you all this, which is not new to you, because I hope you will not give in to being discouraged. You have only been two years in Switzerland and have already achieved the possibility of working there, and of becoming a member of the Swiss Society. This is something which one should not underrate. Even among the Swiss you will in time find people who might join you, but I am afraid that you will have to be patient.

I am keeping well, and, as you see, I am still not // put off, nor shall I be as long as I live. I know that I have been fighting and am fighting for something of the greatest importance. I hope that you can share this conviction and derive courage from it.

With all good wishes

Yours

Melanie Klein

Kl 36, 1-4

Sandridge Park Hotel
Melksham
Wilts
Tel. Melksham 3388

18 August 1958

Dear Marcelle,

Having had a restful fortnight here, I have now at last carefully read and reread your paper Le Temps psych[o]logi[qu]e and enjoyed it very much. Some of your ideas I remembered well from our conversation (when I stayed with you in Geneva) but I found them enriched and very well presented, illustrated as they are by good clinical instances. It is an excellent and interesting paper and gave me much pleasure. I wonder how and when you are going to publish it? You mention that you are going to enlarge it – is that what prevents you from publication? Or have you already taken steps to have it published? I should be glad to see this paper or your Geneva Congress paper published (of course translated) in the International Journal of Ps. A. I remember we spoke about this but I don't know what you decided in the end. Altogether it is a long time since I heard from you and I should be glad to know how you are: personally, your position in conversation with the Swiss colleagues and also your plans for writing; you seem to be full of interesting and fruitful thoughts which should be expressed and published.

I had a busy winter – too many demands on me and altogether I did not feel too well. Nothing serious but a desire to be able to use my remaining strength in the best and most gratifying way – a wish not easily fulfilled. However my book has at last gone to press and after many trepidations and efforts I had a week ago a cable from Boulanger saying that the proofs of the translation have arrived and that he is attending to them. What a relief! In a "Note of the Traducteur" he expresses his thanks to you for the translation of the footnotes and appreciates very much the work you have done.

I feel very grateful for what you have done! It was hard work and [a] good [one] and without your stepping in so willingly, I think the translation would never have been finished! In the autumn, I shall do my best to get French publishers for the other two translations and if I succeed I shall feel a great burden off my mind.

The weather is not good here, but rest and change are beneficial. I hope you have good weather for your holidays and enjoy them fully.

With best wishes

Yours ever

Melanie Klein

Kl 37, 1-2

2/20 Bracknell Gardens
London, N.W.3

19 September 1958

Madame Marcelle Spira
5, Rond Point de Plainpalais
Geneva, SWITZERLAND

Chère Marcelle,

I wrote to you about the middle of August, when I was on holiday, and wonder whether you ever received the letter? I was not entirely sure of your address, so it may have gone astray. I repeat that I said in that letter, that I should like to hear something about you, your work and your position in the Swiss Society. I wonder whether you had perhaps gone to the Congress of Latin-American Psycho-Analysts, of which I have heard some echoes, and had a very nicely detailed description from Baranger. He begs me to visit South America and I wish I could do so, but that is out of the question. I am keeping well, but on condition that I husband my strength.

I have had a pleasant holiday, in spite of not particularly good weather, and am now fully back at work, that is to say, as fully as I can be.

In the letter that I wrote to you in August, I told you that Boulanger has corrected the first proofs, and it was an enormous relief to me to hear that. Now I am writing to Desclée de Brouwer about the Developments and, if I find a publisher for that book, the next thing will be to see about your translation of the Contributions. I need patience for all of this, but, after all, I am not well-known in France, and I cannot be surprised at meeting all these difficulties, but I think that, in the end, I shall get it done.

It will interest you that Dr. Segal is going to spend the whole month of December in the Argentine, which pleases me very much. During the summer, Dr. Gillespie[61], who has had very little contact with my work, and Paula Heiman[n], who gets more and more away from it, were lecturing in Brazil, and Paula Heimann in [the] Argentin[a], and I do not believe that this can have been very useful. I am, therefore, all the more happy that Dr. Segal is going to work in the Argentine. In addition to her qualities as an excellent teacher and representative of my work, she has a very good command of French, which will be helpful.

Here we are already thinking of the next Congress. I have announced a paper; title still unknown, but I am working on it. I shall see where it will lead me. //

In the letter which I am afraid has got lost, I also said how much I enjoyed reading your paper, and how interested I am as to whether it will be translated and where it will be published.

I hope that there is nothing wrong with you and shall be glad to hear from you.

Yours ever

Melanie Klein

---

61 H. Gillespie (1905–2001) was a British psychoanalyst who practised in Edinburgh. He was president of the International Psychoanalytical Association from 1957 until 1961.

Kl 38

20, Bracknell Gardens
London, N.W.3

26 September 1958

Chère Marcelle,

I reply to your letter, which arrived this morning, on the spot, because I have a few moments in which to do so. It was full of interesting news, mixed, of course, because I am extremely sorry about mother's accident, and the difficulties in which it involves you. I was very pleased that you sent your paper for publication and that they have accepted it for the Revue Française. As you know, I have reasons not to wish to get involved with the Lagache group, so I should be all the more pleased if the official review would publish your paper. However, this may take quite a long time.

I was most interested in the results of your clinical work and, although I can see that there is little hope of co-operation with your Swiss colleagues, it may turn out that you will, by and by, find a number of new people who will co-operate with you, which will change the character of the Swiss Society. You may think that I am too optimistic, but actually I have gone through similar experiences myself and, in spite of everything to the contrary, <u>good</u> work does attract some people and those it attracts are usually <u>good</u>.

You mentioned very kindly that you were thinking of the translation of "Envy and Gratitude". I myself consider this book important (although I feel, in retrospect, that I could have enlarged it and thereby improved it). Quite some time ago Baranger suggested translating it and has also, I think, done some work on it.

With best wishes, particularly for your mother's good recovery,

Yours ever

Melanie Klein

Kl 39

20, Bracknell Gardens
London, N.W.3

3 October 1958

Chère Marcelle,

I am sending you a copy[62] of the "Note du Traducteur", which Boulanger attached to the translation of "The Psycho-Analysis of Children". I think you may be interested in it.

Yours in haste

Melanie Klein

---

62 The copy that Klein mentions no longer exists. This is the version published in the book: "Mrs Marcelle Spira participated in the preparation of the Index of this edition and compiled all the footnotes (except for the translator's notes). Much of this additional material is indispensable for a full understanding of the author's ideas. Our gratitude is a tribute to Mrs Spira for taking on the responsibility for translating these." (Boulanger 1959, p. 7) [translated from the original French by David Alcorn]

Kl 40, 1-2

Flat 2
20, Bracknell Gardens
London, N.W.3

18 December 1958

Chère Marcelle,

I need not tell you how I sympathize with the great loss you have suffered. My mother's death has caused me great pain and it took me some time to get over the depression which followed. How often do I think about her even now and miss her – in some ways she remained alive with me! So I know what you have gone through and my thoughts are with you. I did not realize that your mother bad been so ill and therefore did not connect your silence with all the trouble and anxiety you have gone through.

This is only a short note to tell you how I feel for you and with you. I also wish to add my very best wishes for Christmas and the New Year. I am sure you will need a restful holiday. I was extremely pleased to hear how successful you are in your work. Considering the short time you have been at work in Geneva, // this is really a great and promising achievement. It always gladdens my heart to know of success by one of my friends and collaborators and by success I don't only mean external prestige but good work done, conviction and also expression of the work done by writing. Are there among your analysands also future Swiss analysts?

With my love

Your[s] *ever*

Melanie Klein

Kl 41, 1-2

Flat 2
20, Bracknell Gardens
London, N.W.3

1 May 1959

Madame Marcelle Spira
5, Rond Point de Plainpalais
Geneva, SWITZERLAND

Chère Marcelle,

Thank you for your letter of the 25th March. I was glad to see that it gave you so much pleasure that "The Psycho-Analysis of Children" has now appeared in French[63]. To me it is a very great satisfaction – after all, it is the fulfilment of a dream that I have had for the past 27 years. Lagache enquired, now that "The Psycho-Analysis of Children" is out, about the possibilities of placing the other translations, and asked me how far you and Baranger have got with yours. I understand that Baranger has still to revise his translation of The Developments, and it seems that, should he not be able to do it in time, The Contributions may have precedence, but I am aware that you, too, want to do a careful revision, and I know how much work this implies. I take it that you received the "Note of the Translator", by Boulanger, which I think should be considered in any of the other translations. I gather from your letter, and I know it anyhow, that you are extremely busy, but unfortunately there is nothing I can do but ask you whether you are working on this revision and by what date you think it could be finished. I am sure you do not mind my saying that it is better to go slowly and carefully over it, because it is so important to catch both the right meaning and the right French phrase. This, of course, was one of the most important things in "The Psycho-Analysis of Children", which, as you know, I revised entirely and discussed with Boulanger, (except the notes which you made and the Index). It is a great pity that Uruguay is so far from Switzerland and that you and Baranger cannot easily co-operate on certain expressions and the turn of phrases, which I think would be an advantage to both of you. I am sure, if you are in any doubt, Baranger would be helpful.

I was very pleased to gather that you are making your mark on the work in Switzerland and I wonder who the two friends, Kleinian analysts, are who help you. Where do they come from? the Argentine? It would be very nice if you and they came to London in the autumn and I hope that you will let me know in time so that I can arrange as many opportunities as possible of seeing you. You said, however, that you would speak to me about this in Copenhagen. For the first time,

63 Presses Universitaires de France.

I have received a French review from Geneva on my book Envy and Gratitude[64]. I wonder whether this is connected with your work there.

As regards myself, I had a pleasant holiday in England at Easter and worked in a very le[a]isurely way on a paper I am to give to the Anthropological and Sociological Department of Manchester University on the 11th May. They have asked me to address them and have given me full freedom to speak on what I like. Unfortunately, I have left too short a time for this paper, though I do not think that my mental capacity has deteriorated in quality, it has certainly slowed up in recent years. However, I hope to finish next week and shall spend three days in Manchester, where I shall meet various academic people. I am trying, in the paper, to establish links between infancy and later life and the title is "Our Adult World and its Roots in Early Infancy"[65]. I am a bit anxious whether I shall be // able to convey to a University audience, who probably know very little about psycho-analysis, my concept, which I am not diluting but only explaining. Unfortunately, I shall never know whether they understand me, as there will be no discussion and they are very pleasant and too polite to tell me. Anyhow, I shall do my best and, in the course of time, I have got so used to the idea that only part of what I say is understood that I am not too worried about it. After the lecture, I shall take a week's holiday with friends who live near Cardiff, and have a rest, which I shall need, as it is still some time until the summer holidays and in between is the Congress, which is not a particularly restful time. My Congress paper is nearly ready, but I want to go over it again and may still make a few alterations.

I am looking forward to meeting you in Copenhagen and wonder whether your analytic friends will be there. I am staying at the Palace Hotel, so you will know how to get in touch with me. Afterwards, I shall spend a few days in Göteborg to visit my sister-in-law, and from there I fly to Zürich and thence to Wengen, where I shall spend three weeks, very far from work and just looking at the mountains.

This is a very full letter and I hope that you will be influenced by my example and tell me more about yourself.

With love

Yours ever

Melanie

---

64 No extant copy of this review is to be found in the archives of the *Journal de Genève*.
65 Klein, M. (1959).

Kl 42, 1-2

Flat 2
20, Bracknell Gardens
London, N.W.3

16 January 1960

Madame Marcelle Spira
5, Rond Point de Plainpalais
Geneva, SWITZERLAND

Chère Marcelle,

I was very glad to hear from you after this long silence, but the important thing is that the news you give me is good, both as far as you personally are concerned, and the work that you are doing. You have certainly achieved much in the four years, though I know that you have plenty of troubles there, but it is impossible to represent any new work and, in particular, to work better than one's colleagues, without having trouble. I have, in the course of forty years, learnt, not to become indifferent towards misrepresentation or hostility, but to consider that, in spite of all, there is constant progress going on. Believe me, I highly value your efforts, and it gives me great pleasure to hear that the strength you put in your purpose is not diminished.

I am delighted to hear that the translation of my book has nearly come to an end. I take it that this was the second revision, because I understood you to say some time ago that you had gone through it once already. Of course second revisions are most useful. I was amazed, when the publishers returned the manuscript of my "Narra[t]ive of a Child Analysis" once more, in order to avoid corrections in the proofs, how many corrections I had to make in the manuscript. It is a tedious business to go over something again and again, but it pays in the end. I am now expecting the proofs of my book, and I am also writing something which is still in its infant-stage and which should form part of a small book I hope to publish next year.

The "infant stage" brings me to the very good piece of news that you are going to be a grandmother. I send your daughter-in-law my best wishes for a happy delivery. I am sure you will enjoy the baby enormously. The relation between grandmother and grandchild is quite different from that between mother and child, but is one of the great pleasures of life. I am sure the baby will love you. My grandchildren are at an age when they are more or less independent, but I still enjoy contact with them very much. I find that one enjoys, as one did with one's children, their development at every stage.

To return to your translation, I shall only get in touch with Lagache about some help with the publishers when the translation is fully ready. What are you doing about the Index? Are you translating it? Actually this is a very good Index, in contrast to the one in "The Psycho-Analysis of Children", which is bad. By the way, I hear that there is an offer from one of the top American paper-back firms to publish "The Psycho-Analysis of Children" as a paper-back // in the United States. If this comes off, it will be an enormous advantage, because then this book would be read widely in the United States. It will amuse you to hear that my work is referred to in the course of Psychology for students in Cleveland, Ohio, but they are warned that it is not valid according to American psycho-analysts. This seems to have started an urge to read it among some students; they got in touch with Miss Evans[66], who, it seems, managed to impress them. I think that in twenty years, when I shall certainly not be here to see it, the work of my American colleagues will be found to be invalid and my work valid. I hope that my younger colleagues will have the pleasure of seeing this.

I hope you will notice the good example I am giving you of replying so quickly to your letter, but of course I have the advantage of being able to dictate it, and I am not working as hard as you are, so you are forgiven. *I am thinking of spending 3½ to 4 weeks beginning on July 25th or 26th somewhere not far from Geneva but at a height of 1000 – 1200 metres. Could you give me any advice about a* [the] *place or perhaps even about a comfortable hotel? When do you intend to leave Geneva for your holidays?*

With love yours

Melanie Klein

---

66 In 1947, Ms Gwen Evans, who had been analysed by Melanie Klein, was elected a member of the British Psycho-Analytical Society. She later left England and settled in the United States (Betty Joseph, personal communication).

Kl 43, 1-2

Flat 2
20, Bracknell Gardens
London, N.W.3

17 March 1960

Ma chère Marcelle,

I just had your note of 15th and am hurrying to let you know that since time was getting on since I wrote to you first (and knowing that it gets more difficult to find the right accommodation the nearer we get to holiday time) my son got in touch with different hotels through the Swiss agency here. I have booked (just now I received the confirmation) the Hotel Montesano à Villars o/ Ollon. I booked a room from 30th July till 30th August and a room for two days for my grand-daughter who is travelling with me on the 30th. Since these dates are fixed also the aeroplane seats there seems unfortunately no opportunity to see you on my way to Villars. Perhaps on my return on 30th August? I do hope you have not had too much trouble with your enquires, and I regret very much that knowing how busy you are and still uncertain about your own plans, I gave you trouble.

I very much hope there will be another occasion to see you. I am tired but not unwell and it seems that [that] *Villars will be a good place for a good holiday – very much needed.*

Again thanks and love

Melanie Klein

Kl 44

Flat 2
20, Bracknell Gardens
London, N.W.3

25 March 1960

Madame Marcelle Spira
5, Rond Point de Plainpalais
Geneva,   Switzerland
by airmail

Chère Marcelle,

I am very sorry for the mix-up about booking my room. To my first letter telling you about my plans, I had no reply for several weeks. I wondered whether you might be away or busy, and, after two or three weeks, my son thought we might have trouble finding a room in a suitable hotel or in a suitable place, and went ahead with it. Gstaad would, in any case, not have been quite to my liking, and it would also have been a longer journey than I intended. But that is all past history! As soon as I got your second letter, telling me of the trouble you had taken to find me a room, I replied straight away to say that I had already dealt with the matter. As a matter of fact, plans have been altered, as my family insisted on my not travelling alone, and my grandson or daughter (in fact, the former) will travel with me. Accordingly, I have had to change the date to the 30th.

Having had my letter in the meantime, you will know most of what I am saying now, but I am rather concerned about the trouble you have taken, and am also wondering whether you have had to pay some deposit on the room in Gstaad. Will you please let me know, because I should, of course, like to refund the cost. I am quite satisfied with having booked at Villars, which is at the right height, and the hotel seems suitable.

I am very glad that the winter is over. Although I did not have a single cold, I did not feel well, and there were quite a lot of factors contributing to this. I am glad that the spring is coming. I think that my power of recuperation [*is*] [are] still there.

You mentioned in one of your letters that you are finishing, or have finished, the third revision of "The Contributions...". I had a letter from Lagache, asking me how soon "The Contributions..." would be ready. I don't know what Baranger is doing and it gives me great relief that "The Contributions..." is finished, or nearly finished. Will you let me know as soon as possible, so that I can replay to Lagache, who still intends to do something about the publication.

With Love

Yours

Melanie Klein

Kl 45

Flat 2
20, Bracknell Gardens
London, N.W.3

1 July 1960

Madame Marcelle Spira
5, Rond Point de Plainpalais
Geneva, SWITZERLAND

Chère Marcelle,

Thanks for your letter, which was very welcome. I was delighted to hear that the translation of CONTRIBUTIONS...is now ready, but I think it would be better to wait until the autumn before I approach Lagache about a publisher[67].

I hope that your stay in the Argentine will be both helpful and pleasant. Please give my kind regards to anyone I know, especially Dr. Langer[68].

I am writing in a hurry, so I shall only say that I am keeping fairly well, though of course at times I get tired, which is not surprising at my age[69].

With Love,

Yours

Melanie Klein

---

67 The French translation, by Marguerite Derrida, was published in 1968, under the title *Essais de psychanalyse 1921–1945*. It is not known why Marcelle Spira's translation was rejected by the publisher.

68 Marie Glass Hauser de Langer (1910–1987), an Argentinian psychoanalyst, was Spira's analyst in Buenos Aires.

69 Klein died on 20 September 1960, less than three months after her last letter to Spira.

Chapter 6

Six draft copies of letters from Marcelle Spira to Melanie Klein

Preliminary explanations

Regular font – typewritten

Italic font – handwritten

Written in French, the originals of the letters that Spira sent to Melanie Klein are no longer existent. Six draft copies, however, of letters that Spira wrote to Klein were found in the same envelope as those that Klein sent to Spira. Two of these draft copies are typewritten, three are handwritten and the sixth is typewritten with handwritten corrections. The dates and content of these drafts mean that they can be put into the correct chronological sequence; there is, therefore, little doubt that these are drafts of letters that Spira did, in fact, send to Klein.

Various themes are evoked in them: both practical considerations and Spira's own thinking concerning some elements of psychoanalytical theory that she wanted to discuss with Klein. The sections that I found particularly interesting are those in which Spira describes the difficulties that she was encountering in her attempt to be fully accepted into the Swiss Psychoanalytical Society. Klein was very supportive of her in this. It was, of course, something of a surprise for Spira when she discovered how psychoanalysis was practised in the French-speaking part of Switzerland—but it was a surprise, too, for her Swiss colleagues when they discovered the extent to which Klein's concepts were favourably regarded in Buenos Aires. From that point of view, the exchange of correspondence between Spira and Klein is of much more general significance. Those letters show how important it is for us, as psychoanalysts, to make some attempt at working on our disagreements in order to overcome them and to open ourselves up to modes of thought in psychoanalysis other than those with which we are familiar.

Letter #1 from Spira to Klein[70]

5 rue du Vieux Collège
Geneva, 28 October 1955

Dear Mrs Klein,

Your letter, Mrs Klein, was not only a joy to read but also of very great comfort to me.

When I arrived in Geneva just over a month ago, I was hoping to start up a seminar almost at once. I had put forward the idea of doing a seminar on children in Melanie Klein's theory – it was accepted, yet de Saussure seems to have changed his mind and suggests that I start doing it in six months' time. So, I feel as though I'm in a very precarious situation – I do not have any patients, but I am working, and the work that I am doing is very enjoyable: translating "Contributions". I am about halfway through the book in my translation, but I still have quite a lot of revising to do. I will be delighted, Mrs Klein, to send you one of the chapters as soon as possible because that will put my mind at rest and I am grateful to you for that.

I must admit, Mrs Klein, that I am somewhat startled by the kind of psychoanalysis that they practise here in Switzerland. In order to have some contact with my colleagues, I attend various seminars. I contribute as much as I can to the discussions, but, Mrs Klein, "our" way of thinking is like a duck's egg in a clutch of hens. However, although that way of thinking does seem strange to them, they are interested in it. You know better than I do the extent to which your theory can give rise to resistance and anxiety, but even though I am expecting things to be very difficult, I am confident that all will be well.

Needless to say, I was very happy to meet you personally. I really would like to go to London but, financial considerations aside, I think that just now it would not be a good thing for me to do.

As to the difficulties that I am encountering in translating "Contributions" – and you so very kindly offered to discuss these with me – the most recent is as follows: why does a child take so long to process and accept something that he or she has already perceived unconsciously a long time ago? What are the mechanisms that determine whether processing is accomplished more slowly or more quickly?

In the case of a boy with epilepsy, who was in treatment from when he was 2½ to 5 years of age, the heavy dose of Luminal that he was taking from when he was 1 year old meant that his libidinal development was to some extent delayed. This was therefore not regression but a case of developmental arrest (like in Dick's case, but much less severe). Perseveration is a well-known factor in epilepsy and in this little patient it was very visible – he would not go from one kind of play to

---

70 This letter follows the one that Klein wrote to Spira on 21 October 1955 (Kl 1).

another (with water or sand or playing at war) until he had worked through the relevant stage to some extent; oscillations between stages were almost completely absent. That boy's analysis ended four years ago, and he has developed magnificently. His analysis ended earlier than I would have wished; his speech was still very defective, although it had improved. But it was more or less two years later that the overall effect of the analysis really became visible. That would make me think that 1) developmental arrest makes for a very slow process of working-through; 2) in cases of regression, working-through is much quicker; and, 3) rapid oscillations between stages probably lead to almost immediate processing.

This would imply that a fixation point becomes also a means of support. If a child moves forward, he is heading towards the unknown (anxiety-provoking), whereas if he moves backwards, he will have to take underlying anxieties into account. In other words, normal children (with a minimal level of anxiety) should be able to process situations immediately, but they do not. Is anxiety in the face of the unknown or of the problems that every new element of knowledge provokes a sufficient explanation for this?

Mrs Klein, excuse this long letter, but I no longer have any opportunity of speaking "our" language and thank you for listening to me.

I sincerely hope that this letter will find you in excellent health and neither too taken up with or tired out by your work.

Yours affectionately

[*Handwritten signature*]

Letter #2 from Spira to Klein[71]

[Undated; probably written towards the end of November 1955]

[In part typewritten, with many handwritten corrections and additions]

Dear Mrs Klein,

The letter that I received from you yesterday gave me very great pleasure and I thank you very much for it.

I am very pleased by your suggestions both as regards my work and concerning the questions that I asked about working-through. It is true that it is difficult, in a letter, to explain everything that comes to mind. I am at the moment particularly interested in the kind of processing that an artist, in the broad sense of the term, can accomplish through deep-seated regression in the search for unconscious material – recourse to depersonalization such that his ego then becomes able to examine deep-rooted anxieties, take them on board and process them. I think that the deeper the artist's regression, the more universal he is; the more primitive the anxieties, the harder they are to overcome – this goes some way to explaining why the artist's ego may at times be carried along by the id and primitive imagos and thus fall into a psychotic state. That would also explain to some extent the relationship between genius (universalism) and madness, which even to this day is not very well understood. In my view, it is the artist's inability to process quickly enough his anxieties because they fluctuate so intensely – *perception for stable processing is too weak in relation to the dynamics involved* – which is to a great extent responsible for the disintegration of the ego, which at that point is just not strong enough. If he can overcome those anxieties, reinforced as they are by these rapid fluctuations, he will open up his universe more and more and at the same time his ego will become stronger.

That said, I must think again more deeply about your suggestion concerning my work. Nevertheless, I can say right now that I do think that splitting as a defence against anxiety about the object's being lost and destroyed will help me *see the problem more clearly – all the more so since, besides the intense projective identification in this patient, it would explain the high degree of idealization that he has developed, which no doubt is the effect of that original splitting between the good and the bad breast.*

I am at present translating your paper on "The early development of conscience"[72], which will help me in my attempt to understand better that original defensive splitting. I should say that, while I find your paper on "the creative impulse" very moving each time that I read it, your paper on "The early development of

---

71 This typewritten draft with handwritten corrections follows the letter that Klein wrote to Spira on 18 November 1955 (Kl 2).

72 Klein, M. (1933).

conscience" always gives me food for thought. My difficulty lies in the fact that it seems to me almost impossible for the ego to mobilize sufficient quantities of libido in order to overcome the aggressive impulses. If we were to make a drawing, the ego, compared to the id and the superego, would be just a tiny little dot, and the introjection of the good object of the oral sucking stage does not seem to me to be in any way sufficient for overcoming the bad object. Outside of the fusion of the instincts in the first months of life, how does the ego go about this? *For me, non-differentiation between ego and non-ego is not a satisfactory explanation because, from birth onwards, symbiosis is interrupted and is only recovered temporarily during feeding, so that even in its non-differentiated state the ego has to defend itself. Anxiety is present, the hallucinatory situation as surmised by Freud certainly does exist, but the introjection of the original object and the identification that follows on from this forces the ego into a form of* [word illegible] *differentiation, unconscious of course, and into some kind of reaction. I find it difficult to argue that the first three or four months of life are structured only in terms of projection, introjection and identification. The very first introjection of the object gives rise to guilt feelings. I find it difficult to understand how, in the oral sucking stage, the ego does not disappear* [?] *in some form of anxiety-arousing separation* [?]. *In other words, how does the ego survive those first few months of life?*

Dear Mrs Klein, your letters give me great pleasure and your interest in my work is *tremendously* helpful. However, knowing as I do something of your state of health and the fatigue brought upon you by a long life devoted to your own hard work, if it is difficult for you to reply at once, believe me, I will not take offence at that. I, however, did want to answer your letter right away and send my reply to you, together with these three chapters; I hope that, for the readers' sake, you find them clearly written and in conformity with how you express things so profoundly.

It will be obvious, all the same, that I am very eager to hear what you think. I think that I have taken very few liberties in compiling them; where that is the case, my sole aim is to make your concepts as easy as possible for your French readers to understand.

[Draft unsigned]

Letter #3 from Spira to Klein[73]

10 January 1956

Dear Mrs Klein,

On receiving your letter, I really had to ask myself whether it was in fact true that over many years I had analysed my "magical thinking". Before sending my last letter to you, I had written a lot about how difficult it is for me to grasp completely the concept of splitting of the ego in the early days of life. Then I said to myself that such dissertations were not meant to be written down, so I sent you a quite different letter. Your reply, with the enclosed article, was something of a revelation for me. Firstly, I would say that the split between good and bad objects, which have necessarily to be separated from each other, appears to me from what you say to be a need for <u>integration</u>, in the sense of preserving the good object intact. That at last resolved all my doubts concerning the very early ego's ability to face up to the id and anxiety, without having any sense of integration, an aspect that I had found difficult to understand. When we work psychoanalytically, we tend (at least I think so) to forget – because of the countless symptoms and the defence mechanisms used inappropriately – the positive side of the personality <u>from the earliest moments in life</u>. Thanks to your paper, I was able to make a link between the "life instinct" and "integration"; I think that this time, for me, it is not just a case of understanding a concept but of actually assimilating it.

From that point on, the concept of idealization also seemed much clearer to me – but inasmuch as I saw it with respect to melancholic and paranoid individuals. As to your study of criticism with respect to the idealized object, I would say that this is due not only to the sadistic drives but also to the need to discredit the idealized good object with a view to integration; this means that whenever the object is idealized so intensely, it immediately becomes extremely demanding and the superego once more becomes very cruel. In melancholic patients, this criticism by the <u>bad object</u> of the <u>good object</u> is very intense, but if that process were simply intense (I'm incapable, I'm no good, I'm not [two illegible words here]), I would think that projection would be paralysed. I mean by this that criticism does not come only from the sadistic drives; it has also to do with the demands of the idealized good object. This is the case, for example, of the adult who never forgives himself any mistake. In this case, there is certainly a splitting of the object. The good object cannot accept the bad object, and the bad object cannot tolerate the good one (which grows and grows, is idealized, becomes too demanding).

And now I must say that your differentiation between greed, envy and jealousy seems to me to be extremely interesting; more specifically, your concept of envy with respect to the capacity for creativeness opens up a whole new field of action both as regards that capacity in itself – and sublimation, which is still so little and

---

73 This handwritten draft follows the letter that Klein wrote to Spira on 6 January 1956 (Kl 3).

so poorly understood – and from the point of view of the transference. I think too that your ideas will gradually require a whole new review of narcissism (auto-eroticism) and therefore of the psychoses and their capacity for reversibility.

Before I send you back the paper, Mrs Klein, I would like to read it again a few times – but, don't worry, it is in good hands.

Thank you for telling me about your book "New Directions". I ordered it a few days ago, but I hadn't realized that it is a fuller version of the papers in the issue dedicated to you; I worked a great deal on the subject in presenting the case of a female patient in whom writing quite obviously was a mechanism of reparation and recovery.

And now the most secret chapter. I shall begin by telling you that the other day I did a presentation of your theory (part-object relations, the origins of the superego in the light of primitive anxiety) and that your concepts – which, I think, were clearly described – gave rise only to comments that were completely irrelevant; in other words, they spoke about other concepts (Spitz), but nobody criticized or even agreed to talk about what was actually said. Mechanisms such as projective and introjective identification went unheeded. And in my view that is where we should begin. This week, I shall present a case in which these mechanisms are particularly important. There is indeed a lot of work to do; for the people here, the ego seems to be an entity that has no functions of its own, the analytical discourse is based only on content, the transference appears only very vaguely, and the counter-transference does not exist. For example, I heard Krapf [74]

[The letter stops at this point.]

---

74 An Argentinian psychiatrist and psychoanalyst. He was appointed a senior official with the World Health Organization in Geneva. He practised psychoanalysis to a limited extent in that city.

Letter #4 from Spira to Klein[75]

[Undated; probably written towards the end of March 1956]

Dear Mrs Klein,

I'm so sorry for not having replied sooner to thank you for your letters. I have indeed been contacted by Mrs Schüftan[76], and I shall see her at the beginning of April, when she will be in Geneva. She does not mention analysis at all, but the fact of being in contact with someone who has been close to your followers is in itself a very great pleasure for me. And from one particular point of view, there is better news. I now have three patients, which, financially speaking, is a great relief for me; also Krapf asked me not to say anything about it in Argentina, but he will be stopping his work as a psychoanalyst at the end of March, given that he has been appointed to a senior position with the W.H.O. Another analyst, Reding,[77] is going back to Belgium after having lived for quite some time here in Geneva. I imagine that the lack of training analysts will enable me firstly to conduct one of the seminars and secondly to have more patients.

On the other hand, I was very disappointed to learn that Dr Sarasin is opposed to my admission to the Psychoanalytical Society and that "for the time being" the date on which I should be presenting some of my work has been put off until October at the earliest; the reasons for this are, as always, rather vague, but one of them seems to be that "I intended to revolutionize psychoanalysis in Switzerland". I was very relieved at that, and I would so much like him to be right in thinking that I could be capable of doing such a thing.

I am very pleased by what you wrote to me about the translation, Mrs Klein, and of course I am going on with it – at a slower pace, with the hope that your suggestions will prevent me from making similar mistakes in other chapters. I would therefore be very grateful to you if you could let me know as soon as you can what does not seem quite right to you. As you know, I very much want the book to be published in the best possible way. I think also that you will be happy to know that many people over here, who have heard that I am translating your work, regularly ask me how it is progressing and if it will soon be published. Also, on that point, I must tell you that Willy Baranger, who is in Uruguay at the moment, asked me whether I thought that Lagache might agree to have "New Directions" published. It would be wonderful if your works and those of your followers were at last to appear in French; as to that, I think that you might want to get in touch with Baranger and Lagache. I'm sorry that I cannot give you

75 This handwritten draft follows the letter that Klein sent to Spira on 16 March 1956 (Kl 5).
76 See p. 51, footnote 24.
77 Georges Reding was a Belgian psychoanalyst who trained in the French-speaking part of Switzerland and became a member of the Swiss Psychoanalytical Society. He returned to Belgium in 1956, resigned from the Belgian Society in 1957, and later settled in the USA (S. Frisch, personal communication).

Baranger's address because I do not seem to have it for the moment, but it will be easy enough for me to get it from Buenos Aires. I am at present translating the first chapter of your book – it seems to me to be more difficult than the others, although I do not know why exactly.

Dear Mrs Klein, I hope that with the arrival of spring your health will improve. Looking forward to hearing from you

[The letter stops at this point.]

Letter #5 from Spira to Klein[78]

3 May 1956

Marcelle Spira
5 rue du Vieux Collège
Geneva

Dear Mrs Klein,

After sending you the letter in which I wrote particularly about the lectures that de Saussure suggested that I might give, I thought about it again at some length and have come to the conclusion that, taking into account any personal disquiet, it is not really the moment to undertake this kind of thing. I already had those doubts in my mind when I wrote to you last week, but I felt it difficult to share them with you in a letter. Not quite the right moment because, even though I feel that I have managed things quite cleverly here in Geneva, I know that, in other towns in Switzerland, people are still far from convinced of the importance of your theories. Spitz is thought of as having made his mark here and as being very much in personal contact with the overall atmosphere – like Lebovici also. I felt that giving lectures without some more profound and widespread groundwork having been done would only amount to working against the very interests of psychoanalysis such as we understand it and against my own interests too.

That said, I suggested to de Saussure that, since he was going to be in London in a few days' time, he take the opportunity of asking someone from the Kleinian school to come to Geneva (I was thinking of Paula Heimann who, I believe, spends her holidays in Switzerland) to give one or two lectures on child development. I do think, Mrs Klein, that it would be an excellent thing to do and it would have a great impact – at least in Geneva, where the mood is just about ready for something like that and the people are impatient to learn more. I could obviously add that, in my view, it would certainly help me to go on with the task that I have set out upon. It would be an initial close and personal contact that in my opinion could facilitate building bridges…

[The draft stops here.]

---

78 This typewritten draft crossed in the post the letter that Klein wrote to Spira on 3 May 1956 (Kl 7).

Letter #6 from Spira to Klein[79]

[Undated; probably written towards the end of May 1956]

Dear Mrs Klein,

I was so happy to receive your letter – I wanted to answer immediately, but please excuse me for not doing so.

I am delighted that Mrs Segal has agreed to come here; I suppose that in the meantime de Saussure's invitation will have been confirmed. As you can imagine, it was also a great relief for me, because, given that the seminar that I will be conducting this autumn has to do with child development, it will certainly be much easier for me to work on the topic and make it more comprehensible once [H]anna Segal gives her lectures. At present, I am coming under quite strong attack – especially from some "so-called" child analysts – but, contrary to what I feared, the attack is a positive one, in the sense that it is a debate about concepts that are infinitely more far-reaching than those that they have accepted until now.

What surprises all these young women is the fact that an appropriate interpretation calms the child's anxiety and brings in its wake either some new or some more extensive material. One of the criticisms that are addressed to me – and it might be a good idea to tell [H]anna Segal about this so that she can take it into account – is that I interpret without giving the child enough time to associate freely. Even when I point out that the child's play is a substitute for free associations, they see that more or less as something "magical" in a world in which there is nothing to prove that I am right! The fear of coming into contact with the Unconscious is intense; obviously they all should have had a personal analysis – that would seem to me to be a vital necessity in a profession that involves such a high degree of responsibility. I come up against the same difficulty in supervising adult treatments – I keep hearing the question "How do you know that?". Everybody here understands whenever their intelligence is challenged but, alas, they leave their feelings, their affects, and their sensitivity a long way behind. As soon as I came to Switzerland, I felt with some degree of despair just how "intellectual" these people seemed to be.

However, Mrs Klein, although I'm speaking in all sincerity to you, I have no intention of complaining. You are for me hugely supportive and I do appreciate that tremendously. Thanks to you and thanks to the immense support that [H]anna Segal will be for me, I have no fears at all as regards the goals that I have set out for myself. All the same, the news that you shared with me concerning Paula Heimann was more than a surprise – it was a very great disappointment, very painful. I share in what must have been for you some very difficult and painful moments – a situation, as you say, that had been going on for some time.

---

79 This handwritten draft follows the letter that Klein wrote to Spira on 8 May 1956 (Kl 8).

Nevertheless, Mrs Klein, all around you and even far away there are those who are your faithful followers, those who are familiar not simply with your theory and concepts but also with the outcome of these when put into practice. I am often terrified at the idea of Freud coming back to this earth and seeing the extent to which "the dynamics" that lie at the very heart of his life's work have been manhandled by those who think of themselves as his closest followers – 43 years after his paper "On beginning the treatment", they still (for example) give the fundamental rule in its entirety, or interpret only once they know a great deal about the patient's background. For many analysts, Freud's dynamic work has been transformed into a static science – although that in itself negates the very concept of "science". Perhaps, Mrs Klein, one day the world will understand the real meaning of the "depressive position" and come to see that the development of every human being depends solely on his or her capacity to learn how to deal with loss. We all know that it is not easy, but, to quote Charcot, "it doesn't prevent things from existing".

Thank you once again for your very affectionate and encouraging letter. My thanks also to [H]anna Segal, whom I shall soon be able to thank personally. I hope that the coming holidays will give you, Mrs Klein, some prospect of taking a well-earned rest. I send you my best wishes and sincere greetings.

[Signature]

Chapter 7

Facsimiles

20, Bracknell Gardens,
London, N.W.3.

~~TELEPHONE MAIDA VALE~~

~~XXXXXXXXXXXXX~~

18th November 1955.

Chère Madame Spira,

Many thanks for your kind letter. I am
of course delighted to hear that the translation is
progressing but should be very glad to see one chapter.
I am fully aware that revisions will be necessary when
the translation is more advanced, but in the meantime
I might have some suggestions to make which would be
helpful during the process of translation.

I am keeping well, but the pre-condition
is that I do not do too much work and have sufficient
rest. This of course slows down my writing (not to
speak of my correspondence) which I can only do on some
mornings because in the evenings I am not able to do it.
The time is past when I wrote my "Psycho-Analysis of
Children" and most of the Papers you are translating on
evenings or over weekends. This is the reason why
I have only recently read your Congress Paper.

I found this Paper very interesting and it
shows that you are doing good work and have original
thoughts. I was also gratified to find that you seemed
to have very well understood my concepts. If there is
anything I would suggest, it is that it might be helpful
if you described the paranoid-schizoid position (to which
you refer) in a similar way as you defined the depressive
position because some of the conclusions you draw as
regards memory I would also consider from the angle of
the splitting processes in the first few months of life.
The importance of projective identification in the patient
you describe seems to me very great and it might be worth
while to connect your conclusions with the concepts *as well,*
On the whole I enjoyed your Paper very much and was
pleased to meet a colleague who could look so deeply.

I am not surprised that they find you
astonishing in Switzerland, where I believe analysis is

Figure 7.1 Letter from Melanie Klein to Marcelle Spira, dated 29 March 1956,
page 1

-2-

very backward, but the courage and confidence with which
you undertake your task seems to auger well for success.

It would be a great pleasure if you came to
London and we could then have some talks for which the
Congress unfortunately did not allow.   I shall certainly
be very pleased to make any suggestions which would be
helpful for the translation, but there are more and general
points which I should be glad to have an opportunity to
talk over with you, which are not so easy for me to discuss
by correspondence.

However, I shall answer your questions about the
epileptic child as well as I can.   I think this case,
though no doubt very instructive from a general point of
view, is of a specific nature.   As you yourself stress,
there is the perseveration of the epileptic and that may
account for the long period which passed until the effects
of the analysis showed.   I would agree with your suggestion
that this arrested development implies very slow elaboration.
If it is a question of regression the fact that stages
have already been reached in the past makes for a much
quicker result.   Nevertheless, it is true that even more
normal children also need some length of time until they
can work through unconsciously the insight they are gaining,
but the word "working through" is the clue, I think, for
this.   The same applies to adults.   We have again and
again to "work through" material until stabilisation is
achieved.   You know how much Freud thought of "working
through" as a part of the analytic procedure and I am more
than ever convinced that that is the most essential factor.

I need not elaborate on the reasons why the
working through is a pre-condition for successful analysis,
because I am sure you have observed that again and again
defences against insight bound up with anxiety arise.   It
is my belief that the analysis has to take enough time
and there is no prospect whatever, in my view, even if our
technique improves, of shortening it.

We even have to allow that patients after having
finished the analysis, still need a certain period for
settling down, which I think is part of the mourning process

Figure 7.1 (continued) Letter from Melanie Klein to Marcelle Spira, dated 29
March 1956, page 2

-3-

about finishing the analysis.   I have referred to this in my paper on the Termination of an Analysis.

Thank you again for the interest you show in my work and for the great trouble you are taking in translating it, which I realise is a very hard task.

With my best wishes,

Yours

Melanie Klein

Figure 7.1 (continued) Letter from Melanie Klein to Marcelle Spira, dated 29 March 1956, page 3

Flat 2,
20, BRACKNELL GARDENS,
18ᵗʰ December. N.W.3. 5 8

Dear Marcelle,

I need not tell you how I sympathise with the great loss you have suffered. My mother's death has caused me great pain and it took me some time to get over the depression which followed. How often do I think about her even now and miss her – in some ways she remains alive with me! So I know what you have gone through and my thoughts are with you. I did not realize that your mother had been so ill and therefore did not connect your silence with all the trouble and anxiety you have gone through.

This is only a short note to tell you how I feel for you and with you. I also wish to add my very best wishes for Christmas and the New Year. I am sure you will need a restful holiday. — I was extremely pleased to hear how successful you are in your work. Considering the short time you have been at work in Geneva, —

/.

Figure 7.2 Letter from Melanie Klein to Marcelle Spira, dated 18 December 1958, page 1

this is really a great and promising
achievement. It always gladdens
my heart to know of success *achieved*
by one of my friends and collaborators
and by success I don't only mean
external prestige but good work
done, conviction and also expression
of the work done by writing. — Are
there among your analysands also
future Swiss analysts?
With my love
Your ever

Melanie Klein

Figure 7.2 (continued) Letter from Melanie Klein to Marcelle Spira, dated 18
December 1958, page 2

Chère Mrs. Klein,

Votre lettre reçue hier a été un très grand
plaisir et je vous en remercie infiniment.

J'ai apprécié vos suggestions tant en ce qui
concerne mon travail que les questions posées par rapport à
l'élaboration. Mais il est vrai que par correspondance, il est
difficile d'expliquer tout ce que l'on pense. Mon intérêt réside
actuellement, tout spécialement par rapport à l'élaboration suceptible d'être faite par l'artiste en général, qui fait souvent de
profondes regressions à la recherche d'un matériel inconsciant,
mais en utilisant la dépersonnalisation, son moi étant alors capabl
de juger, de voir et d'élaborer les angoisses profondes. Je pense
que plus l'artiste est universel, plus ses regressions sont grandes
mais plus les angoisses à élaboer étant des angoisses primitives,
plus elles sont difficiles à surmonter, et ceci expliquerait
en partie pourquoi l'artiste peut à un moment donné être en traîné
par son ça et les imagos primitives, et tomber dans une
situation psychotique. Ceci expliquerait en partie, la relation
du génie et de la folie, si peu compris jusqu'à nos jours. Je pensais justement que c'est l'incapacité de l'artiste de
faire une élaboratio n rapide des angoisses en raison de fluctuations trop intenses, qui étaient en grande partie responsbables
de cette chute du moi, ou perte du moi trop faible à ce moment là.
Mais s'il peut surmonter ses angoisses, il devient de plus en plus
universel, en même temps que son moi devient de plus en plus fort.

Ceci dit, je penserai plus profondément à votre suggestion
sur mon travail. Quoique dès maintenant, je pense en effet
la morcellement comme première deéfanse contre les angoisses de
la perte de l'objet m'aidera à voir le problème plus clairement,
Je traduis actuellement votre article sur "Le Premier développement de la Conscience" qui m'aidera encore à mieux comprendre
cette première division défensive. Je dois dire que si votre article sur "la pulsion Crétive" m'émeut à chaque fois que je le lis,
l'aticle sur le Premier développement de la Conscience" me donne
à chaque fois de l'angoisse, parce que votre explica-

Figure 7.3 Draft letter Marcelle Spira wrote to Melanie Klein, page 1 (November 1956?)

tion, très réelle, fait penser à un moi presqu'inexistant encore.
Ma difficulté reside dans le fait qu'il me semble presqu'impossi-
bel pour le moi de mobiliser suffisammnet de libido pour vaincre
la force de ses pulsions agressives. Si nous faisons un graphique,
le moi par rapport au ça et au surmoi, semble un point minuscule
et l'introjection du bon objet du stade de suction, ne semble
nullement suffire pour surmonter le mauvais objet. Hors la fusion
des instincts existant, comment le moi s'y prend-il Il semble
que ce serait déjà et uniquement à travers les sentiments
de culpabilité, originant dès un tout premier âge le mécanisme
de réparation. Il m'est difficile de comprendre que ceci n'a pas
lieu déjà dans la phase de suction
Chère Mrs. Klein, vos lettres me font un très
plaisir et votre intérêt pour moi aide certainement à surmonter
les moments actuels pas toujours très faciles, cependant, compre-
nant votre état de santé et les fatigues accumulées au cours d'une
longue vie de travail et de lutte, croyez que si vous ne me répondez
pas immédiatement, je n'en serai nullement affectée. Mais, je te-
nais à vous répondre de suite, afin d'accompagner les troisarticles
que je joins à ces mots et qui j'es père vous semblerons clairs
et d'accord avec votre expression la plus profonde. pour le lecteur

Figure 7.3 *(continued)* Draft letter Marcelle Spira wrote to Melanie Klein, page 2
(November 1956?)

Bibliography

Baer, A. (1950) Le test de Rorschach interprété du point de vue analytique. Trans. M. Spira. *Revue Française de Psychanalyse*, 14: 455–503.

Boulanger, J. B. (1959) Note du traducteur pour la première édition. In M. Klein *La psychanalyse des enfants*. Trans. J. B. Boulanger. Paris: Presses Universitaires de France.

——(2000) Témoignages. *Bulletin de la Société Psychanalytique de Montréal*, vol. 13, 1, pp. 44–50.

Eissler, R. S. (1954) Papers read in the Argentine Psychoanalytic Association: Mrs. Marcelle Spira, Some Aspects of the Analysis of an Epileptic Boy, 107th Bulletin of the International Psycho-Analytical Association, *Bulletin of the International Psycho-Analytical Association*, 35: 379–400.

——(1956) Marcelle Spira, Buenos Aires: Division of Memory, Depressive Position and their Expression in the Course of Transference, Report on the Nineteenth International Psycho-Analytical Congress, *Bulletin of the International Psycho-Analytical Association* c, 37: 118–136.

Ellonen-Jéquier, M. (2008) Personal communication.

Furlong, A. and Bienvenu, J. P. (1994) Jean Baptiste Boulanger: une belle époque. *Bulletin de la Société Psychanalytique de Montréal*, numéro spécial, 7: 60–62.

Grosskurth, P. (1986) *Melanie Klein. Her World and Her Work*. London: Hodder & Stoughton.

Howard, J. (1957) Why Are They Angry? Envy and Gratitude by Melanie Klein. *The Spectator*, 10 August 1957, London: Tavistock Publications.

Jones, E. (1955) *Sigmund Freud: Four Centenary Addresses*. New York: Basic Books, 1955; London: Tavistock Publications, 1956. p. 150.

Joseph, B. (2011) Interview with J.-M. Quinodoz, 24 September 2011. (Unpublished)

Klein, M. (1930) The Importance of Symbol-Formation in the Development of the Ego. *International Journal of Psycho-Analysis* 11: 24–39. Trans. M. Spira. *Revue Française de Psychanalyse*, vol. 2 (1956): 269–288.

——(1932) *The Psycho-Analysis of Children*. Trans. A. Strachey, London: The Hogarth Press.

——(1933) The Early Development of Conscience in the Child. In Sandor Lorand (ed.), *Psychoanalysis Today*. New York: International Universities Press, 1944, pp. 64–74.

——(1946) Notes on Some Schizoid Mechanisms. *International Journal of Psycho-Analysis*, 27: 99–110.

——(1948) *Contributions to Psycho-Analysis*. London: The Hogarth Press.

———(1950) On the Criteria for the Termination of an Analysis. *International Journal of Psycho-Analysis*, 31: 204–204.

———(1957) *Envy and Gratitude.* London: Tavistock Publications.

———(1958) On the Development of Mental Functioning. *International Journal of Psycho-Analysis*, 39: 84–90.

———(1959) Our Adult World and its Roots in Infancy. *Human relations.* 12: 291–303. In M. Masud and R. Khan (eds), *Envy and Gratitude and Other Works 1946–1963.* London: The Hogarth Press.

———(1961) *Narrative of a Child Analysis: The Conduct of the Psycho-Analysis of Children as Seen in the Treatment of a Ten-Year-Old Boy.* The International Psycho-Analytical Library, 55: 1–536. London: The Hogarth Press and The Institute of Psycho-Analysis.

Quinodoz, J.-M. (1991) *The Taming of Solitude: Separation Anxiety in Psychoanalysis.* Trans. Philip Slotkin. London and New York: Routledge, September 1993.

———(2001) *Dreams That Turn Over a Page. Paradoxical Dreams in Psychoanalysis.* Trans. Philip Slotkin. London and New York: Routledge, 2002.

———(2005) Gressot, Michel; Guex, Germaine; Odier, Charles; Réalisation symbolique; Saussure de, Raymond; Société Psychanalytique de Genève; Suisse Romande. In A. Mijolla (ed.), *Dictionnaire International de la Psychanalyse*, Paris: Calmann-Lévy.

———(2005) *Reading Freud: A Chronological Exploration of Freud's Writings.* Trans. D. Alcorn. London and New York: Routledge.

———(2006) In Memoriam Marcelle Spira. *Bulletin Société Suisse de Psychanalysis*, 62: 97–98.

———(2008) *Listening to Hanna Segal. Her Contribution to Psychoanalysis.* London and New York: Routledge.

———(2009) Melanie Klein's Letters Addressed to Marcelle Spira (1955–1960). *International Journal of Psycho-Analysis*, 90: 1393–1418.

Roch, M. (1980) A propos de l'histoire de la Société Suisse de Psychanalyse. *Bulletin Société Suisse de Psychanalysis*, 10: 17–30.

Roudinesco, E. (1993) *Jacques Lacan.* Trans. B. Bray. New York: Columbia University Press, 1997.

Segal, H. (1952) A Psycho-Analytical Approach to Aesthetics. *International Journal of Psycho-Analysis*, 33: 196–207.

———(1979) *Klein.* London: Fontana Modern Masters.

———(2011) Interview with J.-M. Quinodoz, 30 May 2011. (Unpublished)

Spillius, E. (2006) Personal communication by e-mail, 28 August 2006.

Spira, M. (1959) Etude sur le temps psychologique. *Revue Française de Psychanalyse*, 23: 117–140.

———(1963) Intervention au CPLF de Barcelone, 1962. *Revue Française de Psychanalyse*, 27: 223–225.

———(1966) Evoluzione del caso di un bambino epilettico. *Rivista di Psicoanalisi*, 12: 117–152.

———(1983) Création et folie. *Bulletin Société Suisse de Psychanalysis*, 16: 26–30.

———(1985) *Créativité et liberté psychique.* Préface Serge Lebovici. Lyon: Césura, p. 166.

———(1986) "L'impossible" société de psychanalyse. *Bulletin Société Suisse de Psychanalysis*, 22: 25–26.

———(1993) *Aux sources de l'interprétation.* Préface Olivier Flournoy. Lausanne: Delachaux et Niestlé, p. 166.

——(1996) Interview with J.-M. Quinodoz, 21 January 1996. (Unpublished)

——(2005) *L'idealizzazione*. Presentazione Ronny Jaffè. Milano: Franco Angeli, p. 110.

Spitz, R. A. (1946) Anaclitic depression, *The Psychoanalytical Study of the Child*. 2: 313–342.

Storr, A. (1957) Sigmund Freud: Four Centenary Addresses, by Ernest Jones. New York, Basic Books, 1955; London: Tavistock Publications, 1956. p. 150. 18s. *Journal of Analytical Psychology*, 2: 207.

The Listener (Author: unknown) Envy and Gratitude: A Study of Unconscious Sources by Melanie Klein, 27 June 1957, London: Tavistock Publications.

Name index

Index of Melanie Klein's letters

Index of Marcelle Spira's initial drafts